HIKING THE PIONEER VALLEY

30 Circuit Hikes
in the
Connecticut River Valley Region
of Western Massachusetts

by Bruce Scofield

3rd edition
photos and maps by the author

2003
New England Cartographics
North Amherst, Massachusetts
www.necartographics.com

Cover design by Bruce Scofield

Copyright: (c) 2003 by Bruce Scofield
Hiking the Pioneer Valley
    First published in 1991
    Second printing 1993, revised
    Second edition, completely revised and expanded, 1995, 1997
    Third edition 2003, completely revised and updated

Manufactured in the United States of America

Library of Congress catalog card number 03-111467
ISBN 1-889787-09-4

Text and photographs by Bruce Scofield
Cartography, layout and design by Bruce Scofield
Text editing and typesetting by Valerie Vaughan

10 9 8 7 6 5 4 3 2 1   10 09 08 07 06 05 04 03

Attention Hikers!
* Due to changes in trail conditions, the use of information
in this book is at the sole risk of the user.
* Some trails may cross through portions of private land and may not
always be open to the public. Please respect the rights of owners.

---

*Any changes, corrections, comments, or suggestions
about the hikes in this book are welcome.
Send to the author c/o New England Cartographics.*

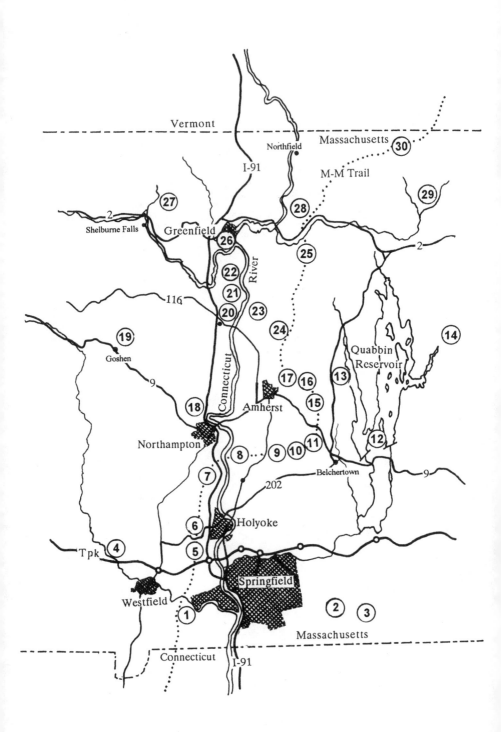

Table of Contents

Introduction

The Connecticut River Valley of Western Massachusetts has been called the *Pioneer Valley* ever since 1938, when the name was created by a regional marketing association. It is an apt name because this was the first interior portion of New England to be settled by the colonists, and it was a dangerous place to live during the original colonization of New England. In fact, a number of Indian raids kept Deerfield and Northfield at the edge of civilization until well into the 18th century.

In the Pioneer Valley we are fortunate to have within easy access a wealth of natural environments to explore on foot. From Connecticut to Vermont, the Connecticut River Valley and the highlands on either side are laced with trails and walkways. A unique geological history has produced tall ridges and mountains towering above towns and farmland, offering first rate views of the countryside. Several long-distance hiking trails also traverse the region, making the Pioneer Valley one of the best day-hiking areas in the country.

Along with the natural features, many of which are described in this guide, the Pioneer Valley has much to offer visitors. Annual events, historical sites, and cultural attractions make this region a worthwhile destination for vacationers in the Northeast. This region is easily accessible from Boston — a two-hour drive west on the Massachusetts Turnpike. Visitors from New York City should take I-95 to I-91, with the total travel time amounting to about three hours. Buses run regularly from both cities, and AMTRAK connects to Springfield as well. If a visitor plans to fly to the Pioneer Valley, the nearest major airport is Bradley International Airport, located between Hartford and Springfield.

The climate of the Pioneer Valley region is typical of the four-season Northeast in general. Visitors should keep in mind that the higher elevations, many of which are explored in this book, may be much cooler than Valley temperatures at any time of year. During winter, snow may fall on the mountains while, only a mile away, rain is falling on the valley towns. Spring can make for some wet and muddy hiking. Hikers should be prepared for wet areas on trails and difficult stream crossings during snow melts or after heavy rains. Summers are warm and often humid. Temperatures in the valley range into the 90s during the day but can drop by as much as 40 degrees during the night. This large variation is due to the fact that the region is inland from the ocean. Autumn is the best season for hiking. Temperatures are comfortable, the insects are scarce, and the foliage colors are striking. The Pioneer Valley offers one of the best fall color displays found anywhere. Winter conditions vary from year to year, although snow may be found annually from December to March, especially at higher elevations.

The hikes described in this book lead to a variety of places, all within a short drive from any location in the Pioneer Valley. They range from easy to strenuous, but this rating is, of course, relative and subjective. Each person will discover for himself how much walking or steep climbing is comfortable and enjoyable. All of the hikes listed here are "circuit hikes" — they are mainly circular; that is, they loop around from start to finish. If you enjoy a walk described in this book, become familiar with it, and then try walking it in the opposite direction. You'll be surprised at how different the experience is.

Before describing the 30 hikes, this book presents some introductory material about the Pioneer Valley. The history of the region, from the remote geological past to the present, provides the hiker with a deeper appreciation of the forces that have created the current landscape and settlement pattern. Following the history is information about the local long-distance hiking trails, the Quabbin Reservoir, the forests and wildlife, and some pointers on hiking itself. This is followed by the main body of the guidebook — detailed descriptions of the 30 circuit hikes.

It has been a pleasure for me to spend so many hours hiking the woodlands and summits of the Pioneer Valley. I hope that this book will introduce others to some of the area's lesser known trails and hiking spots, and stimulate appreciation of the natural world and our responsibility to preserve it.

The Geological and Cultural History
of the Pioneer Valley

Reading the following history of the Pioneer Valley should make hiking the many trails described in this book more interesting and meaningful. From the open summits, views of the Connecticut River, mountains, towns, and farmland will be seen in temporal perspective, and not just appear as postcard images.

Geological History of the Pioneer Valley

The Pioneer Valley has a rich and fascinating geological history, well worth knowing about if you plan to do some hiking. The land here has gone through some very dramatic changes during the past 200 million years, leaving us with a varied and multifaceted landscape. To understand the present landforms we should consider their origins, and this will take us back to the formation of the Appalachian Mountain chain.

Today's geologists interpret most mountain-building to be a product of the collision of continents. Massive plates of land, the continents, float over the hotter and more fluid inner Earth, and they occasionally smash into each other, crumpling their edges and thereby creating mountain ranges. These land masses can stick together and then (possibly later) pull apart. If they do separate, cracks (fissures or faults) form at the boundaries, and one crack eventually becomes the significant division between the two. In our case, three distinct collisions of plates during the Paleozoic era formed the Appalachian Mountains. By the time these mountain-building episodes ended, the world's continental plates became joined, forming the ancient mega-continent that geologists call Pangaea. Millions of years later, as these plates began to pull apart, rifts formed in the area of the present-day east coast of North America. One of these rifts became the Atlantic Ocean; another established the present-day Connecticut River Valley.

It was about 200 million years ago that this major land-shaping event occurred, the rifting of the land that made the Pioneer Valley. Today it is called the Eastern Border Fault. As the land pulled apart, two things happened. First, the eastern and more mountainous side of the rift began to rise, creating a sharp drop-off. Streams and general erosion began reducing the elevations of the mountains to the east, and sand and gravel were deposited into this long basin or depression. The coarser sediments, those that today comprise Mount Toby and the Sugarloafs, accumulated near to the edge of the fault. More refined sediments were deposited further from their source in the form of a large delta. Then lakes formed in this delta region, and these attracted plants and animals, including some early dinosaurs. As the eastern side of the rift valley continued to be uplifted, the sediments which were deposited into the western side weighed it down, and it steadily sank.

Over time, the differential between the two sides was great enough to allow thousands of feet of sediment to accumulate in the rift basin. Because this process was incredibly slow, the cliffs along the eastern side of the fault probably never got too high, perhaps only several thousand feet (this is a matter of debate among geologists), but they certainly must have been dramatic. A painting in Amherst College's Pratt Museum offers a speculative image of how the early Valley might have looked.

The second thing that the border fault created was an opportunity for molten rocks deep within the Earth to seep to the surface. During three separate periods, volcanic magma found its way up through the sedimentary deposits and spilled out onto the plains. In some places, particularly in the Holyoke area, volcanic vents probably formed cones that erupted with some violence. The basalt lavas that covered the land were up to 300 feet thick in places, but because the eruptions did not occur all at once, more sediments were deposited over the flows, creating a sandwich-like effect of lava and sandstone. As the sediments and lava flows piled up in the rift basin, their weight caused the land in the basin to sink further and tilt to the east.

The ancient Pioneer Valley became especially attractive to dinosaurs. As the streams and rivers flowed into the basin from mountains to the east, they brought water which formed life-supporting lakes and mud flats on which the dinosaurs walked. Apparently, the climatic conditions were perfect for preserving dinosaur footprints, because the

9

Valley is one of the world's richest sources for fossilized dinosaur tracks. A major source for tracks which are preserved today in museums throughout the world was the local Barton Cove's "Bird-Track Quarry." The world's only commercial dinosaur track quarry still operates in South Hadley.

When dinosaurs were first discovered and described in the 19th century, Edward Hitchcock, the former Amherst College president and geologist, was known internationally for his meticulous work on dinosaur track classification. Although Hitchcock identified and described 119 different types of tracks and in the process accumulated one of the world's largest collections of dinosaur tracks, he always maintained that they were bird tracks (and this is not too far from the truth, at least from the current scientific perspective on dinosaurs).

The Pioneer Valley dinosaur tracks are those left by early dinosaurs, dating from the late Triassic and early Jurassic periods. Because skeletal preservation in the Valley is very rare, geologists can only speculate as to which animal left which tracks. Most of the dinosaurs were small animals such as the carnivore Coelophysis, though some, including the one that Hitchcock named Eubrontes, were much larger. Current speculation suggests that a 20-foot-long carnivore called Dilophosaurus was the maker of the Pioneer Valley tracks. Later dinosaurs probably inhabited the area also, but the sediments that preserved their tracks have long since eroded.

One of the best places to examine dinosaur tracks is in the basement room of Amherst College's Pratt Museum. (*Note:* as of 2003, Amherst College plans to turn the Pratt building into a dormitory, and the fate of the Pratt collection is uncertain.) Tracks are also visible right where they were laid, along the banks of the Connecticut River where the river erosion has exposed ancient mud beaches. Perhaps the best place to see these is the Smith's Ferry site, owned by The Trustees of Reservations, and located on the east side of Route 5, one mile south of the Mt. Tom State Reservation entrance on Route 5. The site is not marked, but a trail leads from a roadside parking area to the footprint-bearing slabs. Here you can also see firsthand the tilting of the sediments downward toward the east (as described above). There is also a good collection of tracks in the Springfield Science Museum.

In Connecticut, south of Hartford near Rocky Hill, Dinosaur State Park offers perhaps the best preserved prints and some interesting interpretive history. But now, let's get back to the geological history.

Sixty-five million years ago, at the time of a great extinction event that ended the reign of the dinosaurs, the shape of the combined sedimentary deposits and lava flows in the ancient Pioneer Valley was a flat one, called a peneplain by geologists. Only a few highly resistant mountains, including Mt. Monadnock and Mt. Greylock, rose above the plain. But some time later, the land began to rise in what geologists call a broad uplift. The higher the peneplain rose the faster it was eroded by wind, rain, and stream-cutting. Over time and several uplifts, the softer sedimentary deposits were washed out, leaving the more resistant basalt lava flows standing high above the land as today's mountains (the Mt. Tom, Holyoke and Pocumtuck ranges). Only the tops of these mountains preserve the original surface of the ancient peneplain. This same process of sediments and lava flows weathering to form basalt mountains also occurred in Connecticut (near Meriden and New Haven), as well as in New York and New Jersey (the Palisades and the Watchungs).

For a long time, the valley drained to the west, but with the uplifts and deep erosion, rivers changed course and flowed south. By about 10 million years ago, a primary drainage pattern was established and today's Connecticut River was born. The next major valley-shaping event was quite recent in geological time. About 2 million years ago, a series of ice ages began, during which glaciers advanced south from the polar region. The last ice age (the Wisconsin) covered all of New England and extended as far south as Long Island, New York, and Northern New Jersey. Mt. Tom was buried under a mile of slow-moving ice. As the ice slid south, it ground down the summits of the mountains, plucking chunks of rock from their southern faces. It dug into the softer sediments, enlarging gaps and valleys, and it transported this debris further south, dumping it as the glacier began to melt some 14,000 years ago. These deposits accumulated significantly between basalt ridges and created a dam on the Connecticut River near Rocky Hill, Connecticut. The water backed up all the way to Vermont, forming a 140-mile-long lake which geologists call Lake Hitchcock.

Holyoke Range

For at least one thousand years the dam held, and Lake Hitchcock became the dominant feature of the Pioneer Valley. The Mt. Tom and Holyoke Ranges, as well as Mt. Warner and Amherst center, were islands. Streams draining the highlands to the east dumped silt and sand into the lake, forming deltas. One example is just south of Mt. Toby, where these ancient deltas are today's commercial sand pits. The breakup of the dam and the draining of the lake occurred around 12-to-13 thousand years ago, about the same time that humans, the Paleo-Indians, entered the Valley. The lake may not have drained all at once. It is probable that deltas, left by streams emptying into the lake, created small dams that retained portions of the once great lake for many more years. Today, remnants of the lake bottom exist as extensive swampland; Amherst's Lawrence Swamp is a good example.

Cultural History of the Pioneer Valley

As the glacial lakes dried up, small human communities moved into the area to exploit the available food — fish, beaver, and herds of caribou. As the Connecticut River downcut through the old silt- and sand-covered lake-bed, its course became more stable. Flood plains of rich soil were formed, and wildlife patterns became further established and regular. The Valley's earliest inhabitants, the Paleo-Indians, were nomadic hunters. A more settled life-style, based on hunting and gathering strategies, developed by about 5000 BCE, and this lasted for the next six thousand years, no doubt because it was a successful and effective adaptation to the environment. The cultivation of corn, squash, and beans did not begin until about 1000 years ago — a technical revolution that brought cultural change and warfare.

By the time the English colonists began to enter the Valley in 1633, there were major Indian communities established at Agawam, Woronoco (Westfield), Norwottuck (Northampton and Hadley), Pocumtuck (Deerfield), and Squakhaog (Northfield). Apparently, there were loose alliances among these settlements. As a general group they were known as the *Nipmuck*, meaning freshwater Indians, and they had a history of being dominated by the more aggressive Massachusetts Indians to the east and the Mohawks to the west. Although the spread of European diseases had already decimated the coastal Indian population, the inhabitants of the Valley had not yet been affected. Within a few years, however, smallpox epidemics swept through the Valley, resulting in the death of perhaps 95% of the indigenous population. Where formerly there were possibly several thousand Indians living in the region, the epidemic quickly decimated the population, and this opened the way to English settlement.

In 1636, Valley pioneer William Pynchon and a few others took up residence in what is now Springfield, and they quickly began to acquire land from the Indians. Since there were now fewer Indians and plenty of extra land, they parted with it more easily than they might have done so a few years earlier. But there were many differences between the English and the Indians — they had only trade in common. English laws and Indian customs were so different that mutual understandings were very difficult to achieve. The English also distanced themselves socially from the Indians, preventing casual communications of the kind that can cement relationships. The Indians became isolated, unable to actively participate in the changes that were reshaping the Valley.

Pynchon, a shrewd trader, had set up his settlement at the point of northernmost navigation on the river, allowing him to dominate the trading of furs with the Indians. The furs bought from the Indians would be shipped to England or Holland, sold in Russia, or made into hats, which were then sold back to colonists. What the Indians couldn't understand, and what became a source of deep distrust, were price fluctuations of commodities. Beyond this, the notion of credit proved to further compound the problem. The English would extend credit to the Indians, allowing them to buy things, because the main Indian goods (corn and furs) were seasonal. When Indian wars kept the hunters busy, and therefore the supply of pelts low, or when crops failed, credit obligations could not be met. Credit pressure meant selling off more of their land, and this meant less land for crops. The system ultimately didn't work.

It took the English some time to push upriver. The first major barrier was the great falls above Springfield, located in what is now Holyoke. The region beyond the falls, which the Indians called *Nolwotogg* (corrupted to Nonotuck or Norwottuck), meaning "in the midst of the river"), had much fertile farmland. By 1650, pressure to settle and farm this region began to rise, and in 1653 the title to the land was purchased from the Indians and the settlement of Northampton began in the following year. The land which is now Hadley was purchased in 1659, and the local Indians were further displaced.

In 1651 the General Court of the Massachusetts Bay Colony decided to set aside some land, formerly an old Indian burial ground where the Rev. John Elliot preached to the Indians, as a place for an Indian village. Later it was discovered that the town of Dedham had already owned the land. So in 1663 the Court granted the town of Dedham 8,000 acres of land not already tied up in grants to ownership. In 1664 a committee found and selected a place where the Pocumtuck

Indians lived, a place with good soil and access to the Connecticut river. By 1669 plowing began, and Deerfield became the northwestern frontier of New England. Settlers came from Hatfield, Northampton, and Connecticut, but none from Dedham. However, Deerfield turned out to be an unsafe place to live.

In 1675-76 a major war was fought between the Indians and the colonists, generally known as the King Philip War. Philip (his Indian name was Metacomet) was the second son of the great Indian sachem Massasoit. For a number of years the younger Indian warriors had advocated the elimination of the English colonists who were expanding rapidly and taking over former Indian habitat. The situation was really quite bad for the Indians. If they did nothing, they would be overwhelmed and would have to change their ways. If they complained, they were usually held to the standards of the English, who, although they preached to the Indians, would not really allow them to enter into English society. Only Roger Williams and his Providence, Rhode Island, settlement treated the Indians with the understanding and respect that we, living in the 21st century, would expect they should have received.

Most of the action in the King Phillip War took place in the eastern part of Massachusetts. The Nipmucks of the Connecticut River had always lived in a kind of isolation, but they had some allegiance to the Massachusett Indians in the east. As the war became a reality, they were pressured to join the Indian revolt. Older leaders were against this and argued in favor of continuing the tradition of "good" relations with the English. During a group discussion by the Norwottucks on these matters in Hadley, a young warrior killed an older pacifist, and the Indians of the Pioneer Valley joined the rebellion. Within the next year several settlements were attacked, though not destroyed, including Northampton, Hatfield, and Hadley.

In 1673 Northfield had joined Deerfield as a frontier settlement. In 1675, when Deerfield had a population of 125 and Northfield about 100, they were attacked violently by Nipmuck Indians siding with King Phillip. Military men from the fort in Hadley were sent in to handle the matter, but without much success, and Deerfield and

Northfield were temporarily abandoned. These attacks had broken a 50-year peace between Indians and settlers, and tensions ran high in the Valley for some time. Efforts to resettle Deerfield in 1677 failed, but in 1680 the Proprietors of Pocumtuck made a treaty with the powerful Mohawk Indians, and permanent resettlement began in 1682. Another major Indian raid on this town, called the Massacre of 1704, was stimulated by the English/French war declared in 1702. Not until 1746 did the last Indian raid in the Valley occur.

We owe much to those first inhabitants of the Valley. They gave us local names like Connecticut (Quonicticut), meaning Long River. They kept the forests and fields healthy through regular burnings, they introduced the English settlers to many crops and foods, and their forest paths became the roads we now use. Our greatest challenge as a society today is to find a way to relate to the land and to nature as successfully as the Indians did — a difficult task for an expanding and ever-consuming population such as ours.

By the mid-18th century, the Native Americans had been completely displaced, and the Pioneer Valley settled down as a series of small agricultural villages. Soon after the American Revolution, in 1786-1787, a major tax revolt occurred here, the first of its kind in the new country. Since tax collecting was not regulated by the then weak federal government, the states were left with the task of raising money to pay the Revolution's debts. Those in the east of the Commonwealth, mostly Boston merchants, pushed for tax laws that hurt the farmers in the west because the taxes were to be paid in cash, not commodities or barter. The angry farmers, led by Pelham landowner Daniel Shays, protested, eventually attacking Commonwealth troops in Springfield. Shays and his men were fired upon and retreated into the countryside, only to be caught by surprise and dispersed. Shays' Rebellion, as it has come to be known, ultimately achieved its goals (the tax laws were changed) and played a role in the creation of a stronger central government. It is said that Daniel Shays hid with his men and horses in the "Horse Caves" on the north slope of Mt. Norwottuck *(Hike #9)*.

In 1794 Springfield was selected by the federal government as the location for its national arsenal. This moved Springfield to the forefront in matters of weapons technology and manufacturing, and soon the Armory became the city's largest employer. This concentration of manufacturing activity in Springfield gave the Pioneer Valley an early start in the Industrial Revolution. Between 1830 and 1860 a series of railroad lines opened up markets to the Valley that had not existed previously. The ready availability of water power from the Connecticut River at Turners Falls, Greenfield, Holyoke, and Springfield (Chicopee) stimulated the growth of numerous industries, including textiles and papers. Holyoke was, in fact, the nation's first planned industrial city. As an industrial and manufacturing region, the Pioneer Valley achieved many "firsts" and held the lead nationally in the manufacturing of a number of products. Factories were built near river rapids, and water was diverted into canals and brought downstream, above the river level, to turbines that drove the machinery in the factories. Holyoke Heritage State Park, located in the heart of that city's factory district, is an excellent place to learn about the industrial phase of the Valley's history.

In spite of the growth of industry, agriculture continued to play an important role in the Valley's economy. During the 19th century, farmers began to grow fewer but more lucrative crops. Feed grains were grown on a large scale, and apple orchards were started. In the first half of the 19th century, Hadley became the broom corn capital of the world. Tobacco, which had been grown by the Indians and was native to the Valley, began to be raised for profit around this time and continued to be a major crop into the 20th century. The tobacco grown here was used for wrapping cigars; the harvested plants were hung in long, windowless barns which are still seen along the Connecticut River. In the 1880s, Polish immigrants (the first major ethnic group aside from the English) entered the Valley; they stimulated agriculture and actually delayed the urbanization of many areas. These excellent farmers were very successful with onion growing, a difficult enterprise. By 1900, however, it was apparent that small farms were not profitable, and Valley agriculture began to decline more steadily.

By the mid-20th century, the Pioneer Valley had survived many changes in matters of industry and agriculture. The central part of the Valley had become a center for education, and much of the local economy had become dependent on these institutions. In other sectors, manufacturing jobs were being lost, and service jobs were being created. Towns were in decline, suburbs were beginning to sprawl, and things were beginning to look much as they do today. But in the 1960s portions of the Valley were jolted by the federal government into thinking about its future and the land itself. A proposal for a 57,000-acre Connecticut River National Recreation Area was proposed by Senator Kennedy. The plan encompassed scenic lands in Connecticut, much of the land in the Mt. Tom and Holyoke Range area, and also lands in Vermont and New Hampshire. The proposal was soon rejected by the two northern states, and Connecticut wanted total control over its section. Here in the Pioneer Valley, the idea disturbed some of the local towns who feared being overwhelmed by tourists. It terrified private landowners who would have their lands bought out from under them, and it challenged the population at large to think about the future of the Valley's natural resources. The federal plan never materialized, but one result was the acquisition by the Commonwealth of much of the Holyoke Range.

Today, despite the changes wrought by industry and suburbanization, the Pioneer Valley still retains a fair amount of farmland and protected, forested open space. However, environmentally destructive off-road vehicle use has increased significantly, and traffic on major roads is now far in excess of their original design. Developers and development pressure in general continually threaten to gobble up open space piecemeal, with little thought of community impact. When a house is built on an exposed hillside, it is a visual loss for everyone except the owner. Fortunately, many people have come to realize this, and stricter building regulations have slowed down what might have become uncontrolled growth. Today, there is a real need for towns and cities to redirect their local economies and to better organize new construction. It is important for those who appreciate and use the natural features of the Valley to make some kind of contribution to their further preservation. At the end of this guidebook there is a list of organizations that promote conservation, encourage wise use of the land, or actually buy land for preservation purposes.

Hiking in the Pioneer Valley

Within this region, the choices available to day-hikers are many. From the former lake-bottom swampland to the bare-crested summits, a variety of environments are within a short drive. For those interested in longer hikes or overnight backpacks, there are possibilities as well. In this section, we will take a look at some of the area's best hiking opportunities.

The Metacomet-Monadnock Trail

This long-distance foot trail, the backbone of Pioneer Valley hiking, is named for the great Indian chief Metacomet, who fought the early colonists in 1675, and for the spectacular Mt. Monadnock (possibly the most-climbed mountain in the world). Many hikes in this book utilize portions of this 117-mile-long hiking trail as part of the loop. The "M-M Trail," as it is known to hikers and referred to in this text, is always marked with white rectangular markers, often painted on trees and sometimes on rocks. Most of its walkway is footpath or woods road, but there are a few sections where roads are utilized for short distances. It has been routed so that the hiker passes through some of the most interesting and spectacular scenery in the region. Along the way are bare summits, deep hemlock groves, remote swamps, roaring brooks, and waterfalls. An excellent guidebook that offers detailed descriptions and maps for the entire length of the M-M is available and is highly recommended for anyone interested in this important Pioneer Valley trail (see *Sources for Maps* at end of book).

The Metacomet-Monadnock Trail begins in Agawam near the state line of Connecticut (where it connects with that state's Metacomet Trail). From there, it follows the basalt ridges north to Mt. Tom State Reservation. The lava flows of the geologic past, described in the previous chapter, have created a narrow, but lengthy wilderness setting that today lies in the midst of the most populated section of the Pioneer Valley. Locally, the southern sections of the ridge are known as Provin and East Mountains *(Hike #5),* the northernmost being Mt.

Tom and the other summits that lie within the Mt. Tom Reservation *(Hike #7)*. These ridges, composed of basalt, or traprock, have been quarried in places, but still provide a route high above the towns and suburbs. Alongside the ridge are several town watersheds and reservoirs, and also a portion of Robinson State Park, affording some protection to this valuable natural resource.

After crossing the Connecticut River, the M-M Trail turns east, climbs Mt. Holyoke *(Hike #8)*, and then traverses the entire ridgeline of the Holyoke Range (these mountains are also composed of basalt). Next, the trail turns north again, entering a very different environment, geologically speaking. These highlands, part of which are called the Pelham Hills, are composed of ancient gneiss bedrock and are the stumps of a former mountain range whose eroded heights, during the formative time along the Eastern Border Fault, filled the valley with sediments. The M-M Trail climbs into the deep and wide heights of the Pelham hills *(Hike #15, 16, 17)*, and continues north through Shutesbury and Leverett before entering Wendell State Forest *(Hike #25)*. After crossing the Miller's River near Farley, the M-M Trail steadily becomes more of a wilderness trail and traverses ridges and summits, including the 1,617-foot Mt. Grace *(Hike #30)* in northern Massachusetts before crossing into New Hampshire. Its terminus is on the bare rock summit of Mt. Monadnock — at 3,113 feet elevation, it is one of the highest mountains in the area and is visible in the far distance from many of the hikes in this book.

The route of the Metacomet-Monadnock Trail was laid out by University of Massachusetts professor Walter M. Banfield. The route is only partly on public land and continues to exist due to the cooperation of the many state and local conservation and water agencies, wildlife sanctuaries, and private landowners. It is marked and maintained by the Metacomet-Monadnock Trail Conference and the Berkshire Chapter of the Appalachian Mountain Club, which also publishes the official guidebook to this trail (see *Local Organizations* listed in Resources section at the end of this guidebook).

The Robert Frost Trail

The Robert Frost Trail, named for the famous poet that once lived and taught in Amherst, was built and is maintained by the Amherst Conservation Commission (ACC). It totals about 40 miles from the Holyoke Range to Mt. Toby to Wendell State Forest, linking along the way many of Amherst's conservation areas as well as state parks and forests. The markings are orange rectangular blazes, usually on trees or rocks. In two sections, in the eastern portion of the Holyoke Range and in the vicinity of Mt. Orient, the Robert Frost Trail utilizes portions of the Metacomet-Monadnock Trail, so that the hiker will find both orange and white blazes marking the way.

The Robert Frost Trail (RFT) begins near the Notch Visitor's Center in the Holyoke Range State Park, on the east side of Route 116 between Amherst and South Hadley. At first, it heads east on a level route below the summit of Mount Norwottuck *(Hike #9)*. It then joins the M-M Trail east of the summit, just before Rattlesnake Knob *(Hike #10),* and the two trails continue together over Long Mountain and across Harris Mountain Road. After this road crossing, the two trails part, the RFT heading north along a power-line cut. After some road walking, this trail enters and traverses the huge Lawrence Swamp and then winds its way discreetly through several housing developments on protected trail easements before reaching the Amethyst Brook Conservation Area. From here, the trail climbs to the summit of Mt. Orient *(Hike #17)* where it meets and joins the M-M Trail again for a few miles. The two separate for the second time near Atkins Reservoir, where the RFT turns east and heads into North Amherst, passing through the Mill River Conservation Area and around Puffers Pond. Utilizing footpaths, roads, and a railway bed, the RFT reaches the southern end of the Mt. Toby highland at Bull Hill Road. From here to the summit of Mt. Toby *(Hike #23),* the RFT follows a wonderful backwoods route that is one of the most beautiful and challenging sections of this trail. The RFT descends Mt. Toby and travels another seven miles through Leverett and Montague to terminate at Wendell State Park.

The Amherst Conservation Commission (ACC) publishes an excellent guide to the Robert Frost Trail that includes detailed descriptions of each section and topographic maps showing the entire route. The route of much of the Robert Frost Trail is also shown on the topographic Amherst Trails Map, which is available from the town's conservation commission and some area bookstores and outfitters.

The Pocumtuck Ridge Trail

Following the north-south trending ridges along the Connecticut River from South Deerfield to Greenfield, this recently constructed trail is named for the long basalt ridge, Pocumtuck Range, that makes up its bulk. The trail is blazed in blue. At present, some of the land that this trail traverses is in private hands, and the routing is subject to change. *Hopefully in the future, the various local communities and perhaps the Commonwealth itself will play a supportive role in making this 15-mile route more of a reality than it is at present.*

The Pocumtuck Ridge Trail (PRT) begins at the foot of South Sugarloaf Mountain in South Deerfield, then climbs steeply to the developed summit area, famous for its views of the Connecticut River Valley. Continuing its northward journey, the trail descends this hill and then climbs steeply on a very narrow trail to the summit of North Sugarloaf Mountain, where there are excellent views to the west. *(Hikes #20 and 21* utilize portions of the trail in this section.) After crossing Hillside Road, the PRT climbs the long Pocumtuck Ridge, crossing private land where hiking is allowed at the discretion of the land owners.

While the Sugarloafs are composed of sandstone and conglomerate, the Pocumtuck Range is made of volcanic basalt, related geologically to the Holyoke and Mt. Tom Ranges to the south. The popular Pocumtuck Rock, overlooking Deerfield, along with the ski slopes of Eagle Brook School, offer excellent views west to distant hills and mountains (*Hike #22*). Descending from the Pocumtuck ridge, the trail eventually crosses the Deerfield River and enters the Town of Greenfield recreation land, passing over Sachem Head to its terminus just past Poet's Seat (*Hike #26*).

The Quabbin Reservoir

Although there are few marked trails here, the immense Quabbin Reservoir offers exceptional hiking opportunities. *Hikes #12 and 13* are located here; the first being representative of the developed portion of the reservoir, and the second the undeveloped. Many other hikes, including loop hikes, are possible in the Quabbin Reservation. Access is through gates, which are numbered from 1 to 54, and where rules and regulations are posted. The land was once settled here, but is now wild. Unusual bird sightings and encounters with porcupines and other mammals are likely for those that hike here. However, to really appreciate the Quabbin, one should know something of its remarkable history.

The watershed that is now the Quabbin Reservoir was the Swift River Valley; it was created by three large streams that joined in the vicinity of the former towns of Greenwich and Enfield. The West, Middle, and East branches of the Swift River (*Hikes # 12 and 13*) provided abundant water and once supported a small population of Nipmuck Indians. Their name for the area was Quabin, meaning "well-watered place." European settlement of this valley began in the 1730s, and the population continued to rise well into the 19th century. Farming was the primary way of life, with some water-powered manufacturing going on as well. In the mid-19th century, railroads developed all over New England, but they bypassed the Swift River Valley, effectively isolating it. The population dwindled as people moved to industrial centers to find work. Even agriculture was affected because railroads provided access to crops grown hundreds of miles away that were selling for less than those produced by the local farmers. By the 1920s the region had become quite backward in comparison to other areas. Roads were not paved and electricity was not always available, a situation which did not encourage commercial activity. At this point in history, the only bright spot was the discovery of this area by outsiders as a quaint and beautiful place for summer cottages. But all this came too late. The Swift River area had become a powerless yet desirable pawn in a game being played one hundred miles away — in Boston. The game was called "water supply."

The city of Boston has had a long history of water supply problems. Over the years, the growing population of Boston had acquired additional water from its neighboring towns. By the late 19th century, the population was becoming so big that the demand for water would soon outstrip supplies. As the city got bigger, small town politics became impossible, and those who came into power tended to hold onto it and manage the city as if it were a device or machine. A technological elite took the lead in solving the water problems, and these men, entrenched in the bureaucracy and appointed to various boards and commissions, began to look far away from Boston for clean water. These Harvard-educated engineers, supported by the city, first took on the Wachusett Reservoir project and soon after that, the Swift River Valley. Following many years of proposals, hearings and investigations, the decision to create the Quabbin Reservoir came in 1927. By 1939 the work had been completed and the streams began to fill the evacuated valley. By the year 1946, the reservoir was filled.

The construction of the Quabbin was a major engineering feat. It was necessary to build two dams, blocking two gaps in the hills, to stop the waters from flowing south. Tunnels had to be built to divert the streams so that work could proceed on the dams. Since the valley floor was not bedrock but loose glacial deposits, the dams had to extend well over 100 feet below the ground level. Winsor Dam, named for the Chief Engineer of the project, is 2,640 feet long and nearly 300 feet above the bedrock. Goodnough Dike, named for the engineer who, early on, recognized the water-bearing potential of the Swift River Valley, is 2,140 feet long and 264 feet above the bedrock. The present reservoir behind these two dams stretches for nearly 18 miles to the north. The Quabbin shoreline is 118 miles, not including the islands, and the water surface area is 38.6 square miles. Within the reservoir waters lie 60 islands, formerly the hills in the Swift River Valley, which are currently off limits to visitors.

In 2003, there was a new development in the management of the Quabbin. Boston's Metropolitan District Commission (MDC) merged with the Department of Environmental Management to form a new Department of Conservation and Recreation, which now supervises the Quabbin. More information about the Quabbin can be found at the headquarters (located near the Winsor Dam) where there are interesting displays of photographs taken of the old towns, charts showing the changing water level over the years, and information about the Friends of Quabbin Inc., a non-profit group dedicated to the protection of this unnatural wilderness. Maps can also be purchased here, including one of the Quabbin Park area, used in *Hike #12*.

The Forests and Wildlife of the Pioneer Valley

Anyone following the hikes in this book will be walking in a forested environment most of the time. New England is a lush place, filled with herbs, shrubs, and trees. Viewpoints are rare, but they are a real treat after a long walk through a green corridor. Outlined below is an overview of the general forest patterns encountered on the hikes in this guide. No attempt will be made to identify individual tree species.

The forests of the Pioneer Valley fall into three basic categories that reflect the fact that this is a merger zone between two types of forest tree communities. The Appalachian Oak-Hickory Forest is typical of the southern Appalachian mountains and is well represented in this area, particularly in the lower elevations. In some places, the oaks have been hit by gypsy moths, which can be identified by their tan-colored egg cases attached to the trunks.

The second type of forest is the Transition Hardwoods Forest, which is basically a mixture of northern and southern hardwoods. Representative of forests of the northern uplands is the third type, the Hemlock-Northern Hardwoods Forest, composed of hemlock, maple, beech, birch, ash, and white pine. This type of forest is very common at the higher elevations.

Over the years, the composition of the forests in the area has changed. Although the Indians did some burning, much of the forest that the English found was a primeval climax forest of hemlock. Large animals such as bear, wolf, cougar, and eagle were common. By the mid-18th century, the clearing of forests for farmland created a more diverse habitat, and the balance of animal life began to change. By the mid-19th century, nearly 75% of the land had been cleared, and the rest was being logged. Also by this time, many of the larger animals had migrated or had been hunted and killed off.

The industrial revolution changed the economy, and many farms were abandoned during the late 19th century. Pastures and fields reverted to woodland, and the white pine became the dominant species. However, by 1900 the white pines had become valuable again (for lumber), and much land was clear-cut once again. Today, cutting is more controlled and less extreme, and the forests are in the process of returning to their natural conditions. When hikers occasionally encounter a very ancient tree, it is the "exception that proves the rule" — that is, that the age of our present forest is relatively youthful.

The perceptive hiker will notice many signs of wildlife along the trail, such as squirrels and chipmunks scurrying along the forest floor and racing up tree trunks. Grouse may appear with a sudden explosion of flapping wings. Raccoons, porcupines, and skunks will occasionally show themselves, and more rarely, a fox or coyote will be seen trotting away into the woods. Wild turkeys, successfully reintroduced, are also at home in the forest and may be seen walking in groups.

Hikers are more likely to observe more wildlife where two or more distinctly different environments meet. In these "edge" areas, where forest and field meet, deer are sometimes seen grazing close to the safety of the woods around sunset. Downed trees near ponds are often signs of beaver. These animals leave chisel-cut stumps at the water's edge, and they build huge lodges of sticks and mud. In the spring, the chirping of frogs is heard constantly in the vernal ponds and other wet areas. Toads and turtles are also frequently sighted along the trail in such areas. Snakes (usually the harmless garter snakes) are seen sunning themselves, more often in late summer and early autumn than in any other season. Rattlesnakes, typically found in rocky areas, are rarely found in the Pioneer Valley.

Larger animals, such as bear or an occasional wandering moose, are encountered only rarely. However, the huge Quabbin Reservation is a home to such animals and may even be visited periodically by cougar. There are a number of bald eagles that live in the Quabbin, and sightings of these magnificent birds are now actually quite common. Hawks use the Mt. Holyoke and Mt. Tom ridges as markers in their annual migrations, and groups of vultures and hawks can be seen riding the air currents near the ridges during spring and fall.

Plant life along the trail varies, depending on the soil and the amount of sunlight reaching the forest floor. Common large forest plants include mountain laurel, which blooms late in June, and several kinds of ferns. Smaller spring wildflowers include starflower, Canadian mayflower, trout lily, spring beauty, clintonia, lady's slipper, as well as some invasive species. In sunnier areas there are the low-bush blueberry, sheep laurel, and blackberries.

Field guides, such as the *Audubon* or *Peterson* series, will help hikers identify plants and animals; thus enhancing the hiking experience and making it more than just a physical workout. Additional information about local flora and fauna can be found in other guides published by New England Cartographics — *Birding Western Massachusetts* and *Hiking the Monadnock Region.* Those interested in learning more about local wildlife should also visit the Arcadia Wildlife Sanctuary, a Massachusetts Audubon Society sanctuary in Easthampton, or the Hitchcock Center in Amherst. Besides being good places for a hike, they also offer programs led by experts on natural history.

Using the Trails of the Pioneer Valley

Most of the trails utilized in this guide's 30 hikes are marked with colored paint blazes or symbolic markers, usually seen on trees, though sometimes on rocks. A single marker means that you are on the trail. Two markers (one above the other, both usually rectangular in shape) indicate that a turn is imminent and generally the upper marker is placed off center to the right or left, showing the direction of the upcoming turn. In some cases, especially in State parks or forests, signs are posted indicating the name of the trail and sometimes its length as well. In the areas that are not well maintained, markings can often be inconsistent or faded. In such sections, hikers will need to practice good "woods sense" and pay close attention to the guidebook text. Every attempt has been made in this guide to describe the proper route as clearly as possible, and wherever trails have not been marked at all, the reader is warned. However, trails can change over time, so hikers exploring unmarked trails should bring along (and be familiar with using) a map and compass.

An important factor in hiking is conditioning. The hikes in this guide require uphill and downhill walking, which requires the use of muscles that are generally not used when walking on more level surfaces. Those who believe they are in good condition from walking around town may find a short hike up a hill to be a challenge. Similarly, coming downhill (especially down steep inclines) puts stress on entirely different parts of your feet and legs. If you are not sure of your abilities, start with the shorter hikes or those rated "easy," and then work up to the longer ones. While the hikes in this guide are not very long, they can seem so to those who are not in the best of shape.

Trail maintainer on Pocumtuck Ridge

The short description that introduces each hike will alert the hiker to possible problems or complications. Many trails are very muddy in the spring or after a rain, and hikers should be prepared for this. Some trails can be downright dangerous in winter; they call for special equipment, usually cramp-ons or some kind of gripping device worn over boots, to prevent slippage on ice.

Each description in this guide includes a hiking time — a conservative estimate of the length of time most people will need to hike the route described. For some, the given time may be just right for the hike, but not long enough for leisurely rest stops. For others who hike fast, the given time may be too long. Individual hikers will have to determine for themselves how much time is needed to add or subtract from the given time.

Also listed in the introduction to each hike are the highest and lowest elevations which are found along the way. Since large elevation differentials (the difference between lowest and highest elevation) generally mean a good physical workout, this information can also indicate the difficulty of the hike. Where possible, hikes have been routed in such a way that steep climbs come near the beginning of the hike, allowing for a more relaxed finish. Attention has also been given to reaching interesting destinations at proportionate intervals within the hike, and there are indications for appropriate places to eat, rest, and relax.

The maps that accompany each hike are designed to allow you to locate yourself easily along the trails. A scale that indicates both kilometer and mile, and a true north-seeking arrow is provided. The magnetic declination in the Pioneer Valley is about 15 degrees west of north (the needle of your compass should be set to point to 345 degrees). At the time of this guide's publication (2003), about half of the U.S. Government Survey (USGS) topographic base maps used for this book were available only with contour lines in meters (new series), the others with contours in feet (old series). While the author and publisher have chosen to use the latest available government base maps for the areas covered in this guide, the fact is that some of these newer maps are in error. Specifically, some of them show trails that no longer exist or that are not located accurately. Those who are interested in more map features, or in further exploration of certain areas not shown on the maps in this guide, are advised to acquire additional maps, especially those that are made specifically for hikers. All the maps currently available for each hike are listed in the heading, and the sources for each are listed at the end of this book.

Hiking is not so much a sport as it is a multifaceted activity. While it is true that there are extremes on the curve of hikers that might use this book, from trail runners to nature walkers, most are somewhere in between. Good exercise, companionship, the aesthetic appreciation of nature, the study of geology, plants and animals, photography — these are some of the many dimensions of the hiking experience. For whatever reasons one chooses to hike, it is wise to prepare for some of the things that may happen on the trail by bringing along the right equipment.

First on the list of equipment essentials is footwear. Many trails climb over rocks or scurry up loose gravel, and some are very muddy during part of the year. The wrong shoes can ruin a hike. Today's lightweight hiking boots, some with ankle collars and air-cushioned soles, are extremely comfortable and very rugged. These boots can take a dunking, and they have a tread that grips the rock well. In warmer weather, some hikers prefer wearing good quality running shoes. In cold and wet weather, rubber-bottomed boots with leather uppers and felt liners are appropriate. Under icy conditions, often found on the northern and more shaded slopes of the mountains, some type of ice cramp-on is essential. Small, four-toothed instep cramp-ons are inexpensive and can make a slippery descent much safer. In deep snow, snowshoes are appropriate, particularly those designed with bindings on an axle that make climbing easy. Under the right conditions, some trails described in this book may be tried on cross-country skis.

Day-hiking on longer hikes is improved immensely and made safer by carrying a day-pack containing a few essentials. The day-pack itself need not be large, but it should be comfortable and capable of carrying some extra clothing, particularly during winter. In summer, a fanny-pack (lumbar-pack) may be sufficient. In the pack you should always carry a first aid kit, a water bottle or canteen (carry water from home or purify with a filter or iodine), a pocket knife, a map and compass, small flashlight, length of cord or string, rain gear of some sort, tissues or toilet paper, and some food. Each person will also have certain items that they often require such as sunscreen, glasses, or medications. Proper clothing for each season is a must, and a layering system is recommended in which several items are worn and taken off as needed. During the late spring, summer, and early fall, be sure to bring along some insect repellent. Lyme disease, transmitted by ticks, is not common in this area, but every hiker should know something about it and how to prevent it. Information about this problem is available from the Dept. of Environmental Management (phone 617-727-3180) and local public health departments.

Some hikers find it convenient to keep the basic items like the knife, compass, flashlight, etc., in a ditty bag which goes in the pack and can be transferred easily if a different pack is worn. Water bottles, particularly the Nalgene brand, are preferable to canteens. They come in many sizes and are unbreakable and leakproof.

For rain gear, a poncho is usually adequate and can double as a makeshift shelter, although a combination of rain-jacket and rain-pants is much better protection in wind-driven rains. Although plastic ponchos or parka shells are waterproof, they are not very comfortable for long hiking because they keep moisture in as well as out. Some of the newer outdoor fabrics (such as Gortex) can breathe well and are more comfortable for active hiking in the rain, but you will pay steeply to purchase this luxury.

A final word on trails themselves: Trails should never be taken for granted as just somehow *being* there. Somebody, or some group, usually keeps them in good shape and cleans them up on a regular basis. Although a few hikes in this book utilize unmarked and non-maintained trails, most of the loops on pathways are in good shape. Please help to keep them that way. If you are interested in doing any trail maintenance (a volunteer activity that is quite rewarding), contact the AMC or one of the other groups listed in the resources at the end of this book.

Exploring enigmatic stone chamber in the Pelham Hills

Hiking with Children

Introducing children to hiking and nature is something that should be done with some sensitivity. Forcing a child on a hike could leave a negative imprint that will work against the best intentions of the parent. Young children (up to about age 5) should not be expected to keep up with adults from one end of the trail to the other. At this age, they should be allowed to explore the little things they find along the way, and they should be taken to places where they can dawdle for a while. Small streams, waterfalls, and climbable boulders are usually of interest to them. Children this young need to be introduced to the process of exploring nature rather than to the goals of the adult hiker. Sections of *Hikes #2, 16, 18, 26,* and *29* are appropriate for young children.

Once children become familiar and comfortable with hiking (usually around age seven or eight), they may begin to challenge themselves and be capable of finishing longer hikes. Bringing their friends along can make the hiking more enjoyable, and they can be encouraged at this age to lead portions of the hike. Many children enjoy the challenge of climbing up steeper and rocky sections of trail which are found in *Hikes #3, 8,* and *17.* As children grow older and develop a special liking for certain places, allow them to explore alternative trails or even try bushwhacking through the forest.

The Era of User Conflicts

When the first edition of this guide was published (1991), hikers were the primary users of the Valley trails, and mountain bikes (not to be confused with motorized dirt bikes) were relatively scarce. There was some use by horseback riders, but encounters between this user group and hikers were generally friendly — with the exception of incidents involving the hikers' dogs. During the 1990s, however, the number of mountain bike users riding on hiking trails increased dramatically. In certain areas, those using mountain bikes currently outnumber the hikers. Consequently, hikers are warned to expect mountain bikes on some trails mentioned in this book.

The 1990s ushered in an era of user-conflicts among different trail user groups, not just here but across the country. All of this ultimately stems from overpopulation — in simple terms, more and more people want to use the trails now, presumably as a way of relating to nature. There are the birders, the hikers, the hikers with dogs, the mountain bikers, horseback riders, and ATV riders — all competing for the same public land. (Hunters and fishermen also use the land, but are not usually considered "trail users.") As the population grows and more development occurs, the land that is available for outdoor recreation becomes scarcer.

Initially, hikers reacted strongly to the mountain bike phenomena because this user group brings a mechanical device into nature. From the perspective of many hikers, mountain bikes are an "invasive species" that disturb the tranquility of the forest. Few hikers enjoy the experience of having to dodge a hoard of helmeted and uniformed mountain bikers charging downhill on a narrow trail.

Our choice of recreation reflects our attitude toward nature. Hikers are self-propelled, walking quietly through nature and participating in a relatively receptive manner. On the contrary, mountain bikes are promoted as devices that give the rider more power to *conquer* nature. Is nature and the environment something to study, to observe, and participate in passively without seriously disturbing the surroundings? Or should we regard nature as something separate and potentially dangerous that requires conquest? Another question is how much nature can be appreciated while travelling at higher speeds.

Hiking organizations have a long history of trail-building, and in recent years they have seen some of their hard work degraded and more quickly worn down by mountain bikes. With some significant exceptions, such as the New England Mountain Bike Association (NEMBA), mountain bikers have tended to take the existence of trails for granted. It also seems to be popular among some mountain bikers to head straight into any standing water on the trail, regardless of what kinds of water-control, ditches, or bridge work that hikers have invested their time in building. NEMBA has made an effort to address this problem, so hikers on multiple-use trails may notice these initials on bridgework in wet areas. On the other hand, many naturalists and birders prefer to explore nature without any trails at all, and they view trail-building and fast-walking groups of hikers as an intrusion. It may be that hikers are to naturalists what mountain bikers are to hikers. All this may seem relative, but there are limits regarding preservation and the amount of abuse that nature can handle.

Currently, some hiking areas have restrictions on mountain bikes, but these are not always enforced or respected. For example, they are not allowed on the entire Appalachian Trail. Locally, they are not allowed on certain trails built and maintained by the Amherst Conservation Services. The Massachusetts DEM (Department of Environmental Management) has designated some multiple use trails (on which bikes are allowed) in the Holyoke Range and Skinner State Parks. Bikes are allowed (and encouraged) on Northfield Mountain, but not on the footpaths used for much of the length of *Hike #28*. In general, the hikes in this book have been designed for hikers, not mountain bikers, so hikers should encounter few mountain bikes.

It is the opinion of this author that mountain bikes should be restricted to wide woods roads or logging lanes, carriage roads, and the trails that mountain bike clubs have built themselves. Since mountain bikes tear up sensitive trail, they should not be allowed on footpaths, especially ones built and maintained by the hiking community, and bikers should avoid riding during especially muddy periods. One leader of a large hiking club summarized this user-conflict issue when he said, "We don't mind mountain bikers on our trails — in fact, we invite them. We just ask that they leave their bikes at home."

There is another threat to trail quality that has been growing recently; one that makes mountain bike mud-rutting seem tame by comparison. Aggressive marketing of All Terrain Vehicles (ATVs) and dirt bikes, along with the promotion of their power on television, has resulted in a dramatic increase in their usage in Western Massachusetts. ATVs symbolize what has built the current culture (the conquest of nature), as well as the environmentally-destructive aspects of our culture (the insensitive domination of nature). The power of the internal combustion engine within a vehicle designed to withstand severe punishment means serious damage to trails. It is possible that the amount of destruction caused by just one of these vehicles is more than that caused by a thousand hikers being on the trail at the same time. The noise and air pollution that these vehicles produce are another major cause for alarm. (The same can also be said about snowmobiles, but in general, these recreational machines do much less immediate damage to the environment as they don't contact the trail surface directly.)

The first edition of this book (1991) described trails that were small and in fairly good shape. The second edition (1995) acknowledged the impact of mountain bikes on these trails. Many trails described in the current edition (2003) are now so badly damaged by ATVs that I have had to think twice about including them in the guide. I have chosen to include a few new hikes in areas where no bikes or ATVs will be found. But I have also retained a number of interesting hikes that have suffered trail widening and rutting by these vehicles because I think that the hiking community should know what is going on. The hiking community should not be pushed out of the way just because of a few thoughtless and aggressive individuals with their ATVs. Hiking conditions in many parts of the Pioneer Valley today are the worst I've ever seen them, and there is reason to be concerned. Joining a hiking group and communicating with our elected officials is very important for anyone interested in preserving our natural heritage and promoting a life-sustaining, environmentally-friendly use of public lands.

It is important today for distinctions to be made between different trail users, and the first distinction is between motorized and non-motorized. While I am not advocating a complete ban of ATVs and dirtbikes (or possibly snowmobiles), I do think that they pose serious problems for the environment, and they can ruin the experience of nature for other trail users. Those who drive ATVs illegally on trails that are intended for hiking should be liable to a fine of a considerable amount — not a mere slap on the wrist, as is the case now. I should emphasize that I do not oppose users of ATVs pooling their resources and acquiring land on which they can exercise their aggression via machines, but there must be clear and enforced limits to their access on public lands. At present, the Commonwealth allows ATVs and dirt bikes on certain trails in certain state forests and is trying to work with organized user groups. Hopefully, this approach will be successful in limiting the damage that these machines wreak on specific areas of the environment.

30 Circuit Hikes

1

Robinson State Park

Rating: Easy — a pleasant woods walk through a variety of forest and stream environments with a few minor ups and downs. The many intersections with side trails require close attention to the described trail route. Be alert for mountain bikes.
Distance: 3 miles
Hiking Time: 1.5 - 2 hours
Lowest Elevation: 100 feet; 30 meters
Highest Elevation: 210 feet; 64 meters
USGS Quad: West Springfield (old series)
Other Maps: DEM Robinson State Park Trail Map

Except for hearing the occasional sound of cars and trains, hikers in Robinson State Park might not know that they were so close to the densely populated suburban towns of Feeding Hills and Agawam. The park itself, created in 1934 from a donation by a farmer named Robinson, is a relatively narrow band of forest along the south bank of the Westfield River. It is bisected by River Road and also a power-line; portions of each are used in the hike described below. The trails in this 811-acre park skirt the developed sections and follow streams; they penetrate pine plantations and climb embankments, exploring sections that can appear quite remote and peaceful. One trail, not used in the hike described below, follows the bank of the Westfield River downstream for about two miles. Because this park is located in a high population area, the best time to hike here is midweek or during the off-season. Hikers should be prepared to pay a $5 parking fee between Memorial Day and Labor Day. It is possible, however, to park just outside the entrance gate, avoid the fee, and begin the hike on the yellow trail which follows the Westfield River and will lead to the hike describe below. If you choose this option, you are advised to have a copy of the park trail map, and you should expect to add another mile and a half to the hike.

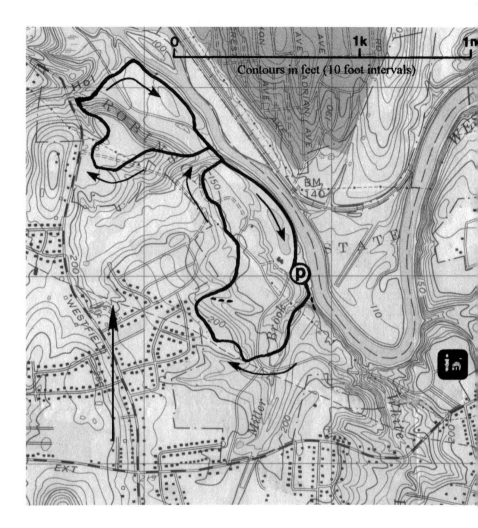

Note: The DEM map of this state park can be misleading because it shows the trails to be color-coded, which they are not. Since 1990 the trails have been marked with official DEM blue plastic triangular markers with symbols, and as of this writing (2003) these markers are applied inconsistently. This may be due in part to the increasing use of mountain bikes on the trails, a use which has greatly accelerated trail degradation. Hikers may now expect to encounter and struggle through wide wet areas (which developed since bike use began around 1990), and should be alert to the sudden appearance of bicyclists.

Trailhead: From I-91, take exit 7 in Springfield, following signs to the Memorial Bridge. Cross over the bridge, and at the rotary, follow route 147 west for 1.7 miles, passing the Eastern States Exposition grounds. Just past where the road crosses over the Westfield River, Route 147 turns right, and then after 0.7 mile, at the second of two closely spaced traffic lights, turn right onto North Street. At this turn, there is a sign indicating Robinson State Park. One mile ahead on the right is the main entrance to the park. A short distance down the entrance drive, just past the toll booth, turn left, then drive one mile on River Road (ignoring two possible left turns) to a parking area on the right near the river. A sign here says Riverside Parking.

Directions: Walk to the far end of the parking area (east) where there is a stone water fountain, and enter the woods on a footpath. A bridge will lead you across a winding brook. To your left is an opening to the Westfield River. Follow the main trail which parallels the brook on its left bank upstream (ignore the other trails heading uphill or towards the river). As of 2002, the trail was marked sporadically and inconsistently with mostly blue and white triangular tags, some with a maple leaf design. The walkway follows the curving brook leading under a power-line, through a delightful hemlock and yellow birch forest and then across a wooden bridge. In this vicinity are the remains of a concrete dam. Follow the path uphill, now leaving the brook (do go back across the second bridge), bear left at the first junction and then right at the second. This leads you to River Road. The trail continues on the other side.

The next section of the trail requires careful attention to the plastic markers (some of which have maple leaf symbols) that usually point in the direction of the turn at junctions. First the trail will come out to an open cut and will follow it for only 100 feet before turning right and leaving it. After a short descent you will arrive at a junction. Turn left here, cross a wet area, and begin a short ascent into a young red pine forest. The trail now approaches the cleared right-of-way of a power-line, parallels it closely for a very short distance and then, as before, leaves it with a right turn. Ahead, the trail passes near a residential area, descends gradually, and reaches a road. Make a left here, just before the road, and follow the path under the power-lines, crossing a road and then a recently modified brook drainage. Berry pickers may find wild fruit growing here in season. About 200 yards past this reconfigured brook crossing, the trail leaves the power-line cut, turning right and downhill, and then turns left after a short distance. From here, the trail follows around the rim of a ravine and then drops down to River Road, the main park road. At the time of this writing, there were a few markers in this last section — at least one with a pine tree symbol.

Turn left on the road, using its bridge to cross over the brook, and then turn left back into the woods, now following blue markers (some with acorn symbols), and going uphill with a view over the ravine to your left. As the trail swings to the right, away from the ravine, it continues to climb, soon reaching the highest elevations of the hike. The trail next crosses the power-lines, re-enters the woods, swings to the right and then makes a sharp right at a junction near some adolescent pines, passes through a pine plantation and then re-crosses the power-lines. All of this is in a relatively remote and beautiful woodland. From the second power-line crossing, the trail meets the edge of a large ravine and descends steeply to a waterfall tumbling over black basalt. (Note that the forest and the trail itself in this steep descent have been seriously degraded by mountain bikes.) A right turn here on the dirt road will lead you along the brook and past a swampy, frog-filled pond to River Road.

Re-enter the woods on the other side of the road and follow the blue markers (keeping left at junctions) to a viewpoint just above the Westfield River. The trail turns right here and parallels the river without approaching it, passing through thick vegetation before arriving at River Road again. Much of this vegetation is invasive species such as burning bush and Japanese barberry. Turn left here and follow the road back to your car. On the way, you will pass trails you used previously, with views of the Westfield River on the left, and Robinson Pond, used by waders. Just ahead, past the pond, you return to the parking area.

2

Laughing Brook Wildlife Sanctuary

Rating: Easy. A stroll through a variety of wooded environments with some ups and downs. Nearly all of it is on footpath with no mountain bikes to dodge.
Distance: 2.4 miles
Hiking Time: 1.5 hours
Lowest Elevation: 330 feet, 100 meters
Highest Elevation: 510 feet, 155 meters
USGS Quad: Hampden 7.5' x 15'
Other Maps: Laughing Brook Education Center and Wildlife Sanctuary Trail Map.

The Laughing Brook Wildlife Sanctuary is a 354-acre property of the Massachusetts Audubon Society. While it doesn't offer much in the way of rugged hiking or spectacular vistas, there are four miles of interesting trails through a variety of wooded areas and alongside or near Laughing Brook. Wildlife viewing is also a possibility, but best of all, you won't see any mountain bikes or ATVs here. Admission to the Sanctuary is $3 per adult (as of 2003), and free to Massachusetts Audubon members. The trails are open from dawn to dusk daily, though not on Mondays, unless it happens to be a holiday.

The original 18 acres of Laughing Brook Wildlife Sanctuary were once the property of Thornton W. Burgess, a naturalist probably best known for his children's books. Burgess (1874-1965) first used his house on the property as a summer residence and eventually lived in it throughout the year. Burgess wrote more than 15,000 bedtime stories and published 70 children's books. Through these writings he established the names of several imaginary animal characters in the public mind; perhaps the best known is Peter Rabbit. Many of the named natural features in the Sanctuary can be found in his stories. Oddly, the name of the brook that runs through the area is not Laughing Brook, it is East Brook on maps. Also located at the Sanctuary is the Laughing Brook Education Center which offers

Common Ink Cap (Coprinus atramentarius)

programs on nature for schools, children, adults and community groups. The Education Center is dedicated to introducing nature to children in various ways. There are many trails near the Education Center that are appropriate for young children and also a number of wildlife viewing platforms. For further information, contact Laughing Brook at 793 Main Street, Hampden, MA 01036.   413-566-8034 laughbrook@massaudubon.org

Trailhead: From I-91 heading south, take Exit 4, and follow signs for Route 83 south and Main Street, East Longmeadow. Make a left at the bottom of the ramp, crossing under I-91. Go straight through a traffic light, and follow Route 83 as it bears to the right on Long Hill Street. After 0.4 mile, turn left onto Sumner Avenue, which is still also Route 83. Pass Forest Park on the right, and after another 0.5 mile Route 83 will veer off to the right. Continue straight ahead on Sumner Avenue, which leads directly into Allen Street, for 8.1 miles to the town of Hampden. Turn left onto Main Street (you may see a sign for Laughing Brook Sanctuary here), drive another 2 miles, and the Sanctuary is on your left. There is a large parking area in front of the Education Center.

Directions: Hikers may want to note that the trail markings at Laughing Brook Wildlife Sanctuary are blue as you go away from the vicinity of the Education Center, and yellow as you move toward it.

From the parking area, walk back out to Main Street, turn right and cross over East Brook. *Be careful - this is a busy road.* Turn right onto the walkway of the first building on your right (the author's home), and follow the brick path around the buildings and up the stairs. At the top of the stairs, find a blue tag and a trail going off to the left. This is the Storyteller's Trail; the named features in this area and near the brook were inspirations for stories written by Burgess. The trail will bear right past a small fireplace and begin to climb, arriving at another small building, a nature study workshop. Continue past the building, and follow the trail along a narrow ridge with a steep drop-off on both sides, following blue tags and blue paint markings. At the first junction, turn left, staying with the markers.

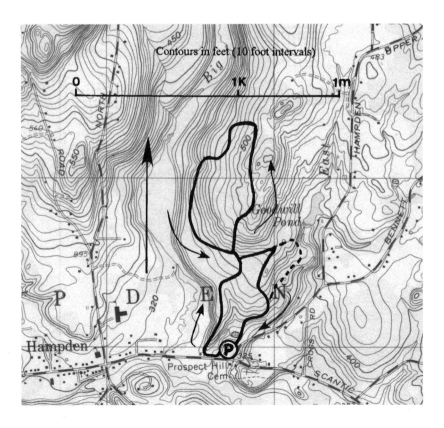

Pass through a pine forest — when the leaves have fallen in late autumn, there may be some limited views to the west of a parallel range of mountains. The trail will then swing around to the right in a section of forest with a ground cover of lycopodium, which resemble miniature trees with brown buds on top. Old rock walls are also found in this section where the trail skirts a wet area. Soon you arrive at a 3-way junction. A marker here points to north. (For a shorter hike, turn right here, and follow the directions below — skip the next paragraph).

Leave the Storyteller's Trail at this 3-way junction, and turn left on the Neff Trail. After only 50 yards, you will arrive at another junction, this being the point at which the actual Neff Trail circuit begins. Turn right here, heading toward the highest elevation of the ridge. On its gradual rise, the trail wanders through a forest of Eastern Hemlocks, some of them quite large. It's not much of a climb, but some rock outcrops along the way make it interesting. At the "summit," you will enter a small patch of more open oak forest. Continue north on the trail, crossing through a rock wall and re-entering a hemlock and pine woods. The trail may be wet in places here after heavy rains or snow melt. Soon the trail turns back on itself (keep left at a junction with a small footpath), then it begins to descend through a very dark, mature hemlock woods. You should be following yellow markers now, which indicate that you are heading back toward the Education Center. After a bit of wandering through evergreen forest, the trail descends and arrives at a flat area that was once a pasture. Rock walls mark its boundaries. Soon the trail turns abruptly left, up and away from this former farming area, reaching another level area dominated by mostly large white pines. The large coarse-barked pine on the left side of the trail is a pitch pine, identified by its bark and 3-needle clusters. After one more small rise, you will arrive at the junction where the loop began. Turn right and walk the 50 meters to the junction with the Storyteller's Trail; then turn left.

Continue following yellow markers along a small rise. There is a rock outcropping and then a large glacial erratic on the north side of the trail. Just ahead and a little downhill, you will come to a junction with the Green Forest Trail. Turn right here and follow the wide path through a beautiful white pine and oak forest. Just a short distance ahead is a fork in the trail. Bear left to the large split boulder where there is a bench — a nice spot for taking a break. When you are ready to hike again, another short path will lead you back to the main trail. Continuing in a southerly direction, follow the trail as it descends. You may begin to hear the sounds of traffic on Glendale Road. At a junction with the Lone Little Path, turn right and head downhill through a large rock wall to another junction near East Brook. (You may wish to explore this area and follow the trail upstream.) To continue, follow the path along the brook, heading downstream, and bear left at the next junction, crossing the brook on a large wooden bridge. Now follow a gravel path in an open area past a small pond (Smiling Pool) where (in 2002) a beaver has taken down many trees. You are now in a heavily-used trail section of the sanctuary, just in back of the center. Observation platforms are found nearby. The Education Center is ahead, and beyond that is the parking area.

Lycopodium clavatum

3

Peaked Mountain

Rating: An easy-to-moderate loop hike to several outstanding vistas atop Peaked Mountain.
Distance: 2 miles
Hiking Time: 1.5 hours
Lowest Elevation: 760 feet, 232 meters
Highest Elevation: 1,227 feet, 374 meters
USGS Quad: Monson 7.5' x 15'
Other Maps: Trustees of Reservations Peaked Mountain

The Trustees of Reservations is a member-supported conservation organization dedicated to preserving areas of special natural and historic interest in Massachusetts. The organization was founded in 1891 and has been a model for later organizations such as the Nature Conservancy. Many of the properties managed by The Trustees have much to offer hikers (two others are described in this guidebook). Membership is recommended; contact Membership Department, The Trustees of Reservations, 978-840-4446; 572 Essex Street, Beverly, MA 01915-9973.

Peaked Mountain, pronounced "pea-kid," is one of the most recent additions to the 94 reservations currently managed by The Trustees of Reservations. Concern for preservation of this area began in 1985, following a fire on the mountain. An organization of several landowners was formed, and they constructed woods roads that would allow emergency fire vehicles onto the mountain in the case of another fire. This association, the Peaked Mountain Co-op, allowed public access to the mountain, and they covered their costs with firewood sales. The several woods roads that traverse the mountain, used as walking trails today, were named after these original landowners and their relatives. In 1999, The Trustees of Reservations acquired the property which totals 297 acres. Not all of Peaked Mountain is protected today, but adjacent to the southeast boundary of the reservation is a 530-acre conservation area owned by the Norcross Wildlife Foundation.

Looking south from Peaked Mountain

In times past, wood from Peaked Mountain was used to make charcoal. Timber was first cut and stacked to dry, then many cords of wood were set on end in a circle, with an opening in the center. This circular wood-pile was covered with soil and the center section was ignited. For days the buried wood pile would burn very slowly, and any flames were quickly extinguished by charcoal tenders supervising the process. The result was charcoal, an excellent lightweight fuel used in the days before coal and oil. Hikers may notice the remains of charcoal mounds in various parts of the reservation.

There are actually two sections of the Peaked Mountain reservation. The mountain itself is located on the portion traversed by this hike. The other section is located roughly 1/2 mile to the northeast, just off Butler Road, and is centered around Lunden Pond. A parking area is located here, and trails lead around the pond.

Hikers will notice that, in addition to the fact many of the woods lanes and trails are named for people who were involved in the preservation of Peaked Mountain, the markings in the reservation are not consistent or well-organized. Names not on the map may appear along the way, and it may seem that the same trail has more than one name. It will help to follow your route on the map provided at the directory, or on one downloaded from The Trustees of Reservations website, so that you may be able to account for any possible discrepancies between reality and the text at this time of writing (2003).

Trailhead: From Laughing Brook Wildlife Sanctuary (see directions for Hike #2), continue east on Main Street, and go straight ahead onto Scantic Road. Drive another 0.5 mile, and turn left onto South Monson (there is a sign here for the Springfield Sportsman's Club). Follow this road for another 2.5 miles, then turn right onto Butler Road. The parking area is just over one mile ahead on the left, just after the end of the pavement. There is room for about 20 cars.

From Route 32 in Monson, drive west on Bliss Street, then turn right at Oak Street Junction. Continue through the next intersection to Lower Hampden Road. Three miles ahead is Butler Road; turn left and drive just over one mile to the parking area.

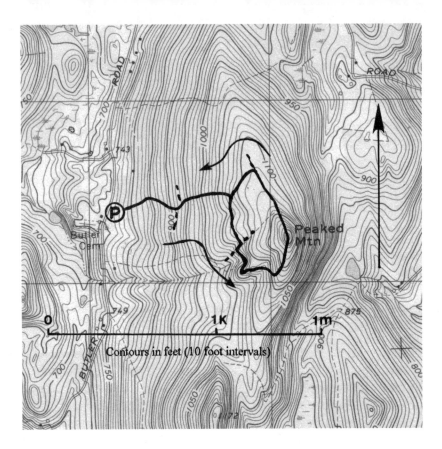

Contours in feet (10 foot intervals)

Directions: From the parking area, walk east to the directory (there may be maps stored here and an opportunity to make a donation — please do). Continue past the directory through the field, and enter the woods on a wide path named Roslyn's Turnpike. This lane is well worn, no doubt due to usage by motorized vehicles in the past. It climbs steadily uphill and soon comes to a junction with Kevin's Road where there is a tiny pond complete with frogs and cattails growing along its sides. Stay to the left at this junction, following signs to Peaked Mountain. You will soon pass a wide lane on the left (Skid Row), and further along you will arrive at a T-junction. On the map this lane is called Bernie Ave. There is a bench here and signs for Peaked Mtn (a left turn) and Valley View (right). The plan is to make a loop around the mountain top from this point, so turn right and follow the lane, which is apparently also called West Rock Trail, past the remains of an old charcoal mound.

Continue along the trail which descends a bit, then arrives at a junction with another woods road (Red Inn Road). Turn right here, now following blue markers, and continue the descent — but only for 150 feet. Be prepared to make a left on a footpath (Valley View Trail), following signs to "Valley View." (If you miss this turn, you will soon see signs noting that you have reached the reservation's boundary.) This footpath passes through an oak forest and then through a stand of mountain laurel. Follow the blue markers over rocks, now climbing more steeply to an overlook of exposed bedrock. This vista is called Valley View. In front of you to the east is Boulder Hill, a north-south ridge, and beyond that in the far distance is the city of Springfield.

From these ledges, continue following the trail, which now turns left into the woods. It leads you through a forest of oaks, maples and blueberry bushes, and will soon come to another rocky area. More climbing is needed before you arrive at another ledge, this one with views to the southeast. Enjoy the view, then continue climbing over a series of small ledges to arrive at the main summit at 1227 feet, along with its 180-degree vista. Peck Hill is to the east. To the north are the hills of the Quabbin with some of the reservoir visible. The Holyoke Range north of Granby is also visible at 30 degrees west of true north. There are two USGS markers are here, one reading 1896 on the brass cap. There is also a mailbox with a hiker's log in it, which may make for some interesting reading!

Leave the summit, following the heavily used rocky path, down through oaks and huckleberries. The trail is not marked, but its route is obvious in spite of the fact that it is braided, possibly due to ATV abuse in the past. When you come to a junction, make a right turn, and further ahead you will pass Ruth's Mountain Road on the right. At the junction with the Valley View Trail (where you were earlier), turn right, and continue your descent on Roslyn's Turnpike. Stay on this road, ignoring all side trails, to return to your car.

4

Tekoa Mountain

Rating: Difficult for several reasons: limited access, few markings, and serious ATV damage. A challenging hike featuring a significant vertical rise, the need to locate unmarked trails, and a steep descent over rugged cliffs. Rattlesnakes, an endangered species, live on this mountain.
Distance: 3.5 miles
Hiking Time: 2.5 hours
Lowest Elevation: 250 feet; 76 meters
Highest Elevation: 1122 feet; 342 meters
USGS Quad: Blandford 7.5' x 15'
Other Maps: Tekoa Mountain Wildlife Management Area

Tekoa Mountain is the rugged, bare-ledged mountain that is visible on the north side of the Massachusetts Turnpike just west of the town of Westfield. It is located in the towns of Montgomery and Russell. The mountain rises abruptly above the Westfield River waterfalls, near the buildings of the Strathmore Paper Company mills (now closed). Just a few years ago, the mountain was owned by the paper company. Today, a large piece of the western part of the mountain is the Tekoa Mountain Wildlife Management Area. Portions to the east are owned by the Springfield water department or are privately owned. Access to this tract presents problems, and only experienced hikers are advised to explore this mountain. Be advised that hiking conditions on the mountain are subject to change. The hike description below may need modification in the future.

Because trails on the mountain are not officially maintained by any public agency or hiking association, there are few marked trails. The USGS Blandford topo map does show a few jeep trails, but these represent only a percentage of those that actually exist on the mountain itself. For the most part, the network of woods roads on the mountain, including those on the summit ridge, are used by dirt bikes and ATVs. The hike described below is, for the most part, off these muddy roads and located on footpaths that may not be well-marked. Other sections of the hike require good woods sense. It has also been reported that rattlesnakes, an endangered species, are sometimes seen on these sunny cliffs. *If you encounter a rattlesnake, do it no harm, and leave the area immediately.*

Tekoa Mountain is obviously not a hike for beginners. In spite of its potential difficulties, this is a spectacular ridge to hike on, and the graffiti scars on the cliffs, while visible from the turnpike, are not so obvious from the mountain itself. In between sections of the struggling pitch pine forest high on the ridge, which has suffered from a series of recent fires, Tekoa Mountain's bare rock outcrops offer excellent views to the south and east.

Fire on Mt. Tekoa, April 1994

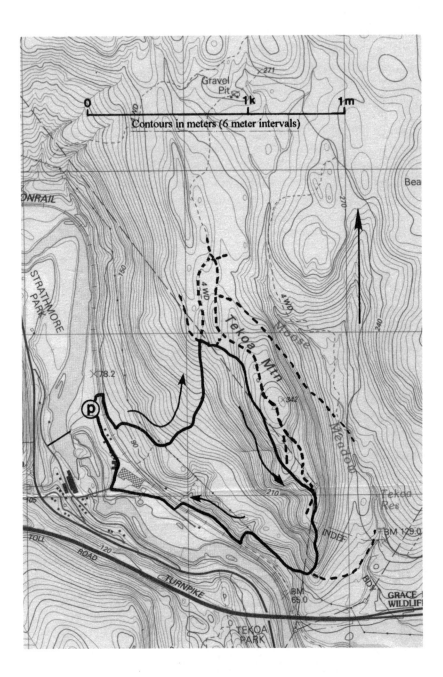

Trailhead: From exit 3 on the Mass Turnpike, follow Routes 10 and 202 south for 1.5 miles to the junction with Route 20 West. Turn right here onto Route 20, following signs to Russell and Pittsfield. After 4.6 miles, Route 20 will pass under the turnpike where you see the bare cliffs of Tekoa Mountain rising directly in front of you. After another 0.5 mile, turn right onto Woronoco Road. Proceed past the mill buildings, and turn right onto the one-lane bridge going over the Westfield River. After crossing the bridge, and before passing any houses, there is a grassy, unpaved lane turning off to the left. Park here — there is room for only two or three cars.

Directions: From your car, walk through the overgrown lane (watch for ticks) for a short distance north to the railroad tracks, cross the tracks, and scramble up the slope on the other side to find a dirt road that parallels the tracks. Turn right onto this road, and head south. In less than 0.1 mile, turn left onto a rocky, badly eroded lane that heads uphill. This woods road, while easy to follow, has some deep ruts from ATV and off-road vehicle use, and these may be channels for running water during rains or melts. After a steady uphill climb, you pass a trail coming in on the right, and just after that, one on the left. Continue straight ahead on the lane which climbs relentlessly uphill for the next half mile, passing a descending lane and then a marked footpath which crosses the trail.

A left turn here climbs and explores a small ridge, offering some vistas. To continue the hike, turn right and follow this lightly-used footpath (known locally as the Unkamitz Trail) as it travels east and then south through scrub pine and oak, burned forest, and over bare rock slabs. Gradually, the trail climbs toward the highest point on the ridge. This footpath, which is marked (but may be hard to follow in places), runs more or less parallel to a major woods road, desecrated by ATVs, that is located a short distance to the east. Markings are not always consistent and may be hard to follow. After cresting the high point of the ridge, the trail descends and crosses the lane near a large glacial boulder.

Follow this descending footpath south along the eastern side of the mountain's ridge. There are excellent views out to Mt. Tom and Springfield from an open ledge along the trail. You can also look back to the jutting peninsula of the mountain that you were just on. Further south along the trail, you will come to a side trail going off to the right which also leads to a clearing and many fine views. During the fire in April of 1994, this small clearing did not burn, and we found it filled with birds and wildlife that were escaping the heat of the flames.

Staying with the marked, south-trending footpath, begin your descent of the eastern section of the ridge. Follow the blazes, and be ready for some very steep sections. Ahead and below are the turnpike and a sand quarry. You come down to a small notch where you should be alert for a sharp left turn. A short rise here takes you through a particularly scenic section of bare rock and pitch pines reminiscent of mountain ridges in Maine and northern New Jersey. With the turnpike almost directly below you, the trail begins its final descent off the mountain and enters a deciduous woods. Look for the trail to swing to the right. The path will head west, come to a power-line clearing, and then swing to the north following the power-lines. This narrow, winding footpath will descend and then arrive at a rather vague junction where you should turn left, dropping down to the service road that parallels the tracks. Turn right onto this lane and head north.

After a 10 minute walk on the fire road, you should reach a point where it swings to the left, approaching the tracks. Cross the tracks here, walk 150 feet to the north, and find an opening that leads left to the paved road. Turn right onto the road, and walk north, past and around the mill, past some houses, and find the unpaved lane where your car is parked.

5

East Mountain

Rating: A relatively easy hike on the crest of a narrow basalt ridge and alongside a reservoir. There are a few short but steep uphill sections, and trails may be muddy due to abuse from motorized trail vehicles.
Distance: 3 miles
Hiking Time: 2 hours
Lowest Elevation: 430 feet; 131 meters
Highest Elevation: 680 feet; 207 meters
USGS Quad: Mt. Tom (old series)
Other Maps: Metacomet-Monadnock Trail Guide

East Mountain is the long basalt ridge that runs due south of Mt. Tom to Westfield. It is related geologically to the Mt. Tom and Holyoke mountain ranges. East Mountain is not as high as Mt. Tom, but it displays many of the same characteristics, such as a narrow summit ridge and steep cliffs on its western side. The hiking trails in this area, including the Metacomet-Monadnock Trail which follows the summit ridgeline, are mostly on old woods roads. Unfortunately, dirt bikes and ATVs have done significant damage to these roads in recent years. In response to this, trail maintainers have relocated sections of the original route onto footpaths, but even some of these have been appropriated by the motorized users.

Protection of East Mountain, a valuable stretch of wilderness adjacent to major population centers, is limited. Much of the area traversed by this hike is on Holyoke watershed and reservoir land. Further south, the ridge, called Provin Mountain, is shrinking as it is quarried away for road pavement. It is important that concerned hikers be aware of the problems that threaten local natural areas and to be supportive of their protection and preservation.

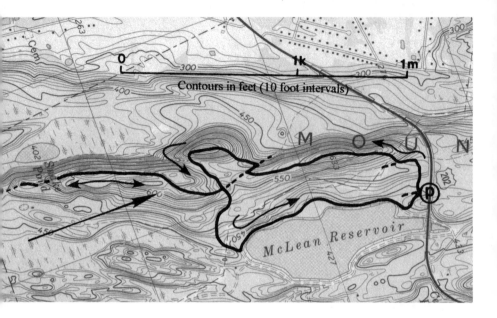

Contours in feet (10 foot intervals)

Trailhead: From exit 16 on I-91, follow US-202 south for about 3 miles (toward Westfield). Immediately west of the McLean Reservoir, which is visible to the left and marked with a sign, the Metacomet-Monadnock Trail crosses US-202 at the height of land. Park near the crossing (there is space for a few cars on either side of the road), or closer to the reservoir, where there is also space for a few cars. *Be very careful* here because US-202 is a busy highway.

Directions: Begin this hike by following the white markers of the M-M Trail on the south side of the highway. The marked trail enters the forest on a woods road and quickly turns right alongside a chain-link fence, one that has been unsuccessful in keeping out ATVs and motorized dirt bikes. The trail parallels US-202 for a short distance and then swings to the left, climbing the ridge of East Mountain. The climb is gentle, but steady and very interesting. Alongside the trail are "glacial erratics," which are boulders carried by the glacial ice sheet of the previous ice age and dropped in place during the melt. Most of the boulders are composed of the reddish Sugarloaf sandstone (arkose), yet they rest on the basalt bedrock. You pass a clearing for a buried telephone cable before reaching the high point of this section of the ridge. There are a few pine-shaded overlooks along this section that make good, non-abused areas for rest stops during the climb.

Ahead, the M-M Trail descends slightly as it continues south. You will reach a more heavily used dirt road on which the trail turns right — but only for a few feet. Be prepared to make a quick left turn onto a footpath that heads downhill and then climbs, steeply in places, the next ridge.

As you near the top, you will be presented with a horrifying example of what just a few individuals on motorized trail vehicles can do to a natural environment. As of 2002 the devastation was quite extensive. From here, the trail swings to the right and up to the bare ridge with its steep cliffs. The vista, which looks west and takes in Buck, Horse and Pequot Ponds of the Hampton Ponds State Park, is quite expansive, but this area has also been abused. However, you can find some privacy and cleanliness just to the north or south of this main viewpoint. When you leave the area, still heading south on the M-M Trail, pay close attention to the trail markers which turn left at a fork and lead to a steep descent. At the bottom of the descent, turn left, and follow the white markers northeast, ignoring all the ATV trails, until you reach a major junction. The M-M Trail turns right here, while a trail marked occasionally with blue markers turns left. From here, you can continue on the circuit hike or take an extended side-trip. (See **Extended Hike** below.)

To continue with the circuit, follow the blue markers along a dirt road, which can be quite muddy at times. (In the past, this route was the old M-M Trail; the relocations have moved it up to the ridge — the way that you came.) The road soon veers right at a heavily rutted junction, then winds around and descends to the reservoir. Turn left here and follow the blue markers south on the service road, with the shoreline on your right. (In 1994, much of the forest along the shoreline was logged.) Further ahead, the service road meets the waters and hugs the shoreline closely. At the end of the reservoir, just after the point where the road swings right, blue markers on a rock point to the left. The trail, which may be unclear at first, leaves the road just before a rock outcrop and arrives in about 200 yards to a junction with the M-M Trail near the highway and your parked car.

Extended Hike: If you are enjoying the vistas and would like to explore a more isolated and remote area, turn right at the junction with the blue trail and continue following the M-M Trail south. (In 2002, this section of trail showed damage from ATV usage.) After an initial uphill climb, the trail soon becomes more interesting. You pass a long, narrow vernal pond caught between two ridges and then walk over slabs of glacially polished bedrock. After about 0.5 mile or more, you reach several vistas overlooking Snake Pond. For the return, retrace your steps back to the junction with the blue trail. If you take this side-trip, add an extra 45 minutes to your hiking time.

Starflower

6

Holyoke Community College

Rating: Moderately challenging — several steep climbs and some sections with unmarked or hard-to-follow trail.
Distance: 5 miles
Hiking Time: 3.5 hours
Lowest Elevation: 400 feet; 122 meters
Highest Elevation: 770 feet; 235 meters
USGS Maps: Mt. Tom (old series)
Other Maps: New England Orienteering Club Recreation Map 5; Holyoke Community College Trail Guide, M-M Guide.

Holyoke Community College is set against a ridge parallel to another that is traversed by the Metacomet-Monadnock Trail. On the back (western) side of the college are two trailheads that allow access to a large tract of interesting ridges, cliffs, and vistas. A 1.3-mile system of marked trails are accessed from this trailhead. The trails of the Holyoke Community College Trail System were created in 1975 as a class project directed by Dr. Winston Lavallee. The trail system was improved by students in 1993, with a trail guide and map produced by student Gary White as an honors project. The guide, which gives detailed descriptions of the vegetation along the trail, is available from Michael Giampietro, Director of Facilities, Holyoke Community College, 303 Homestead Avenue, Holyoke MA 01040. In the area beyond the college trail system, logging and ATV use have made some sections more difficult to navigate (due to removal of trail markers or complete destruction of the trail bed), and hikers will need to pay close attention to the terrain when off the marked trails.

Trailhead: From I-91 take exit 16 (Holyoke/Westfield), and follow signs for US-202 south and Holyoke Community College. Just after the exit, be alert for a sharp turn south. After less than one mile from the exit, turn into Holyoke Community College, and make a left onto Campus Road. Travel along this perimeter road, keeping left past the

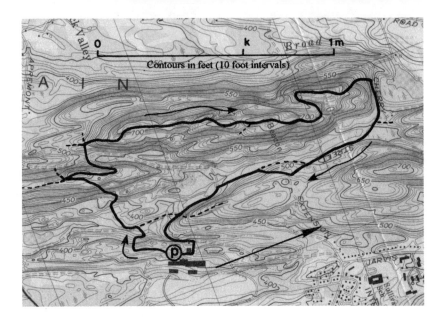

campus center, and around to the back of the college. On weekends, a good place to park is in the lot opposite the sign (on the left) for the college trail system. The trail system sign reads "Do no dishonor to the earth lest you dishonor the spirit of Man," a quote from Henry Besten. You may also continue driving around the back of the campus to a visitor parking area located just past the campus police station. From there, walk the short distance back to this trailhead.

Directions: From the trail system sign, follow the rock-paved path up the slope. You'll notice that the path diverges into two trails almost immediately. Stay to the left, following yellow markers. After a few minutes of trail walking on a small ridge through oaks and mountain laurel, the trail turns right and heads downhill towards a brook. (Ignore another trail coming in on the left, and be alert for a sign indicating that the trail has been relocated.) Just before you reach the brook, the trail turns right, paralleling it for a short distance before crossing it on planks. After the brook crossing, the trail meanders through an area that was logged in 1994. You may wish to take a short-cut here by leaving the trail and bush-whacking a hundred feet or more due west to reach a substantial woods road on which you should turn left. If you do not take the short-cut, continue following the yellow markers, and you will eventually meet this same woods road onto which you should turn left.

64

Now heading south on the logging road, be alert for a right turn (west) onto another unmarked woods road at a point just before a brook crossing. This unmarked road (wet in places) climbs the ridge ahead of you in a few switchbacks. Just past an old stone wall that joins a large rock outcrop, the trail makes a switch to the left. As you approach the crest of this hill, do not descend the steeply eroded ATV trail. Instead, turn right on the white-blazed M-M trail, and walk up to the grassy, cedar-studded clearing for some excellent views. East of the ridge, the Westfield airport is visible, and to the south is McLean Reservoir. To west is the next ridge that you'll be climbing further along on this hike.

Follow a narrow path north along this scenic ridge but be prepared for the white markers to turn suddenly left from the ridge. Here the markers lead steeply down a basalt talus slope (watch your footing!) as the trail swings to the south. The route skirts a wetland on your right when it levels out. Bear right, and directly cross a sandy lane which once served as the Holyoke-Westfield streetcar trolley route. Climb straight ahead on a moderately steep skid road for a short distance to a 4-way intersection. Turn right here, heading uphill in a northerly direction. The white markers will bring you to the top of the ridge where there are excellent vistas immediately to your right (east). After a short uphill scramble further along the M-M Trail, there are views to the west. Either vista makes an excellent spot for a rest or snack. It is possible to reach this point in the hike in under one hour walking from the parking area.

Continue heading north, following the white markers of the M-M Trail which stays close to the edge of the ridge. You'll pass several scenic overlooks amongst twisted cedars, hemlocks, and a few white pines. Ahead, the trail passes along more cliffs and wanders through forested low points on the ridge. In one quite spectacular section, the trail follows a needle-like extension of the ridge with sheer drops on either side. From here the trail descends, winds around, and meets a dirt road. The white markers lead left here, and they will bring you to a high point on the ridge where an old beacon tower stands. Here you may also find evidence of ATV use and ritual beer-drinking activities.

Continuing north along the ridge, the trail descends through a picturesque pine forest, passing a remarkable glacial erratic of conglomerate sitting on basalt. This stone was probably transported via glacial ice sheet from the Sugarloafs many miles to the north.

Watch for a sharp left turn where the trail begins a descent into a saddle between ridges. Keep left; do not go straight uphill here. The trail now doubles back on itself and penetrates a remote area that is shaped like a bowl. In parts of this section, the trail may be overgrown with bushes — pay attention to the markings. A short but stiff climb will bring you to the southernmost extension of the ridge. Here are exposed rocks and good views, making this another good spot for a rest; it is the last really good vista on the hike. From here, continue following the M-M Trail north, across the last section of open ridges on this hike. Mt. Tom and its summit "antennae farm" looms ahead of you. Many of the oaks in this area are dead, the results of devastation from gypsy moths in past years. More recently, ATV abuse has widened the route. At the end of the ridge, the trail veers left, leaving the ATV lane, and descends very steeply. A swing to the right brings you to a gravel road onto which you should turn right (Cherry Street Extension).

The M-M now follows the road and swings around to the south. (Note: a recent private land closure has required a major relocation of the M-M Trail in this area.) Pass the Holyoke Revolver Club, and then pass through a gate entering Massachusetts State Fish and Wildlife land. The road heads gradually uphill, becoming more primitive but also showing signs of illegal dumping, as well as ATV and dirt bike use. Where this road swings to the left, look for an unmarked lane that comes in on your right. Turn right onto this lane which immediately veers left and heads south, descending to the level of a brook, meets a lane coming in on the right and then passes through a section in bad shape — the large mud puddles may require detours. Next, at a T-junction with another road, bear left. After about one-quarter mile, you will reach a gate and a clearing (a staging area for a lumbering operation in 1994) blocked by barriers. At this point, you have two choices.

A right turn here on the Pipeline Trail takes you, via yellow markers, downhill and across a brook on planks and then to a footpath that parallels the logging road. This is the Holyoke Community College yellow trail that you followed at the beginning of the hike, and it leads back over the brook again and then uphill. After climbing, it swings left, heading north, and eventually arrives back at the trailhead on which you began your hike.

The second option is to follow the yellow markers of the Holyoke Community College trail system straight through the open area (a left turn here on the HCC Ridge Trail leads to a vista) and then back into the woods. The markers lead through a small but scenic glen, and then they turn right, off the lane, leading to the visitor's parking lot near the campus police station. If you didn't leave your car here, walk out to the main drive, turn right, and walk back to your car.

7

Mount Tom State Reservation

Rating: Strenuous — a moderately long hike with two steep climbs and some cliffside walking. The views are outstanding.
Distance: 6.5 miles
Hiking Time: 4.5 hours
Lowest Elevation: 165 feet; 50 meters
Highest Elevation: 1,115 feet; 340 meters
USGS Quad: Easthampton-Mt.Tom, Mt. Holyoke (old series)
Other Maps: NEC Mt. Tom, NEOC Mt. Tom, M-M Guide

This hike is a grand tour of Mount Tom State Reservation. You will walk through some beautiful forests, observe a waterfall, climb an observation tower, and gaze over the spectacular cliffs of the main ridge. The trails are all marked and kept in good condition. Because the hike begins with a stiff climb to Goat Peak and then another steep climb of Whiting Peak, it is rated strenuous. It should also be noted that the cliffs are steep, potentially dangerous, and not for hikers who are afraid of heights. But for those in good condition, this is an excellent hike that should be taken on a day with good visibility. During September and October, the cliffs of Mt. Tom are an excellent location for watching the annual hawk migration.

There is an old story about how Mt. Tom and Mt. Holyoke got their names. Among the first English explorers of the Valley, back in the 1630s, were Elizur Holyoke and Rowland Thomas. The story goes that these two were crossing the Connecticut River between the two ranges. Elizur Holyoke, having reached the east bank, shouted to his friend that the mountain ahead would be named Mount Holyoke. Rowland immediately responded by announcing that the mountain behind him would be called Mount Tom.

Today's Mt. Tom State Reservation was established in 1903, one of several state-owned tracts that were to be managed by the counties in which they were located. Forerunners of this type of arrangement were the Mt. Greylock and Mt. Wachusett reservations. Apparently, the counties of Hampden and Hampshire had some differences of opinion regarding the goals and costs of preservation, and a number of compromises had to be reached. Much of the mountain ridge was eventually acquired, except for the southeastern section which was owned by the Mt. Tom Railroad company that had a line running to a hotel on top of the mountain. This tract is the former Mountain Park and Mt. Tom ski area. Today, the reservation occupies 1,800 acres, and since 1990 has been managed entirely by the Massachusetts Department of Environmental Management.

There are many trails in the Mt. Tom area, including the white-blazed Metacomet-Monadnock Trail which follows the main ridge line in a south-north direction. Other trails are marked in various colors and are indicated in places by signs. The local chapter of the Sierra Club and other hiking groups have been responsible for maintenance of these trails. The Mt. Tom Reservation is very popular, and the trails are well-used on weekends. If you desire more solitude, hiking on a weekday in the off season is recommended — and parking is free. On weekends and holidays, however, a $2-per-car fee is charged for entrance to the reservation.

Trailhead: From exit 18 off I-91, drive 3.4 miles south on Route 5. Turn right onto Ferry Road, which is marked by a Mt. Tom State Reservation sign and enters the reservation just after passing beneath I-91. A booth is located here, and a fee is charged on weekends and holidays during the summer and autumn. Just past Lake Bray, about 0.25 mile ahead, turn left off the main road into a large parking area. Park anywhere here.

Directions: Notice that the parking area is part of a loop that swings back to the main road. Walk out of the parking area to the main road, turn left, and walk about 0.2 mile uphill to the trailhead of the red-blazed Tea Bag Trail — on your right near a wooden guard rail. Signs here and elsewhere in the reservation identify the trail and indicate

69

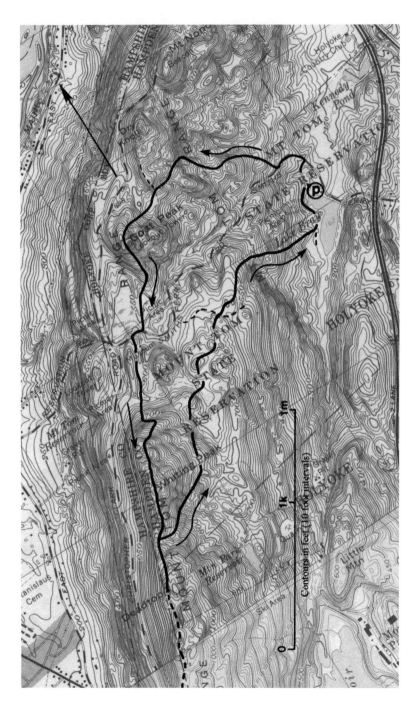

distances. Follow this footpath as it continues the uphill climb, now through a hemlock and laurel forest. You will soon pass a small waterfall splashing over black basalt below you to the right. Ahead, the trail skirts the edge of a small cliff, then drops down to cross a tiny valley. After a relatively level stretch through a section of hardwoods and laurel, the Tea Bag Trail meets the Metacomet-Monadnock Trail. Turn left (south), and follow the white markers.

From the junction, the M-M Trail climbs steadily toward Goat Peak, crossing a service road on the way. The summit area, which was cleared in the winter of 1991-92, offers some good views to the west over Easthampton and the mountains that form the valley walls beyond. Better views are found due east of the M-M Trail from an observation tower on the true summit of Goat Peak, elevation 822 feet. From the tower you will see the massive bulk of Mt. Tom with its antennae farm dominating the south side. Holyoke, Springfield, and distant Hartford are to the left of Mt. Tom. To the northeast, the continuity of the ridge of the Holyoke Range is evident, the river's gap not seeming quite so wide as it appears from other perspectives.

To continue the hike, return to the M-M Trail and follow its white markers south, now descending on a rocky footpath that soon brings you back into shade of hemlocks. Just before reaching the paved park road, the trail utilizes a wide lane that passes underneath a stately group of large hemlocks and white pines. The trail turns right onto the park road and follows it a short distance, past the museum entrance, before turning left onto a woods road. After passing a maintenance yard at the Quarry Trail junction, about 0.25 mile from the road, the trail begins to climb Whiting Peak very steeply on rock steps. After a switchback, the grade lessens and the path approaches the western escarpment of the ridge with its vertical cliffs of columnar basalt and outstanding views over the valley below.

For the next mile or so, the M-M Trail follows the cliffs past a succession of viewpoints, each one unique. Use good judgment in this *potentially dangerous area* because the vertical drop is considerable. Notice how the cliffs are actually columns of basalt, some standing apart from the cliff proper. The top levels that the trail follows have been flattened and polished by the glacial ice sheet.

Columnar basalt on the cliffs of Mt. Tom

After cresting Whiting Peak, the trail gradually drops down to a trail junction. Make a note of this location as you will be returning here to complete the circuit. Continue heading south on the M-M Trail past this junction. The path will climb, and in places scramble, over rock out-crops to another high point in the ridge, this one called Dead Top (elevation of 1,115 feet). Here are the widest and most open views yet encountered on the hike. Just before reaching a boulder, the trail turns right and down, swinging around to another dramatic overlook. After taking in the scenery, return the way you came, back to the trail junction in the low point between Dead Top and Whiting Peak.

[**Optional Extension:** Continue south on the M-M Trail to the summit of Mt. Tom where a mountaintop hotel once stood, but is now replaced by communications equipment. To return, retrace your steps to the trail junction noted above. This optional extension will add nearly 2 miles and an hour to the hike.]

At the junction, you'll notice two red trails meeting the M-M just a few feet from each other. Take the second (northerly) one, labeled the D.O.C. Trail, which heads roughly northeast. The trail descends a hundred feet or so, enough to block the winds, and then follows a contour for a distance. Gradually, the trail drops lower and lower, snaking its way over and around the glacially smoothed outcrops of bedrock. After just under a mile of walking you come to another junction. Take the Keystone Extension Trail, directly ahead and also marked red, across a brook on a bridge and into a hemlock forest.

For the next 0.7 mile, the beautiful Keystone Extension Trail winds its way through hemlocks, along the edge of a swamp, and around boulders and outcrops. It ends at a 4-way junction where you should turn right onto the Keystone Trail, marked intermittently with wooden red keystones. This trail, one of the oldest in the park, descends on a wide path through an open yet shady hemlock forest. It may be wet in a few places, but it is always passable. Just before reaching Lake Bray, visible through the trees, the trail ends. Make a left here, now following yellow markers, and walk out to an old parking area. Keep walking north on pavement along the shore of the lake to the main parking area and your car.

8

Mount Holyoke

Rating: Moderate, with reservations. It is a climb, with a few steep sections, on mostly graded former carriage roads to the Summit House with its commanding views of the Valley.
Distance: 3 miles
Hiking Time: 2 hours
Lowest Elevation: 210 feet; 64 meters
Highest Elevation: 935 feet; 285 meters
USGS Quad: Mt. Holyoke (old series)
Other Maps: NEC Holyoke Range State Park: Western section, M-M Guide

Clearly visible from I-91, Mt. Holyoke is the mountain with the "house" on top. This westernmost summit of the Holyoke Range has long been a popular destination; its excellent views of the Connecticut River Valley, as well as nearby and distant mountains, have attracted visitors for two centuries. Weekends often bring crowds to the summit, so hikers desiring more solitude should hike during midweek.

Mt. Holyoke has the distinction of being the site of this country's first mountain-top inn. Back in 1821, a single room structure was built on the summit, and by mid-century the "Prospect House," as it was called, had become very popular and was seeing a succession of renovations and additions. During the early 20th century, plumbing, electricity, and other conveniences were added to the operation, but the heyday of mountain-top resorts was winding down. The famous New England Hurricane of 1938 did much damage to the hotel, bringing an end to commercial hostelry but also a beginning of State park status. It was in that year that Joseph Allen Skinner donated the mountain and the Summit House to the State. The mountain and the house are now within Skinner State Park.

Besides the Summit House, which is now only a portion of its original size, there is also the Halfway House, located below the summit and linked to it by an extremely steep clearing. When the Summit House was in full operation, guests would arrive by carriage at the Halfway House where they would enter a covered tramway that would take them directly to the summit. Pictures of this elaborate mechanism are on display in the Summit House itself.

Although there is an easier way to reach the summit of this mountain (by car), the hike described here offers a far more interesting visit. The paths utilized are mainly old carriage roads that gain elevation gradually. The final 250-foot climb to the summit on the M-M Trail is steep, however, and so is the descent to the Halfway House. These sections should not be underestimated, and some readers may find this hike quite a challenge. Since the hike climbs and descends the mountain on its northern face, hikers may encounter ice or snow that lingers on the trails longer than one would normally expect. Slippery, even dangerous conditions may present themselves. Winter hikers should probably carry crampons, particularly for the steep descent.

Trailhead: From Route 9 in the center of Hadley, a mile east of the Coolidge Bridge, turn right (south) onto Route 47 and follow it for 3 miles. Just after a point where the road swings to the right to parallel the mountain ridge, you will find a parking area, a gate, and a sign for the Halfway House Trail on your left. (Note: This parking area is also 1.8 miles south of where Bay Road turns left off of Route 47.)

Directions: Walk through the gate, and enter the woods on a trail marked with both blue and pale-yellow markers. The trail rises gently at first, but quickly levels off and descends a few feet. Be prepared to turn left onto the Taylor Notch Trail, following only the pale-yellow markers. The markers will lead you to a well established lane which the trail follows for a short distance before turning right onto another lane. Here, amid mountain laurel and hemlocks, the gradual climb to the summit begins. With the exception of a few level stretches, the climb is mostly a steady uphill walk on a wide lane through the shade of green hemlocks. The last section, just before the summit road, is steep and travels over loose rocks.

Walk straight ahead on the summit road for only 150 feet or so, and then turn right onto the white-blazed Metacomet-Monadnock Trail which immediately heads steeply uphill on steps made of railroad ties. After this first stiff climb, you will reach a more or less level section that leads through a tunnel of clustered hemlocks and white birch — a real contrast to the previous section. Ahead of you now is the last climb, a steep one, that leads to the eastern end of the developed summit. From here to the Summit House you will find a series of excellent views to the north from dramatic rock outcroppings. Discreetly located picnic tables invite a rest and a snack or meal. The white markers of the M-M Trail will lead you through this picnic area to the Summit House itself.

The Summit House is open during the summer season (May-October) and offers the visitor a glimpse into the history of this scenic mountain retreat. Views are possible from its several levels, including one on the roof. Along the veranda are strategically located vista maps that enable you to identify distant features, including Mt. Snow to the north in Vermont and Hartford to the south in Connecticut. Restrooms are located in the lowest level, accessible from the eastern end of the building.

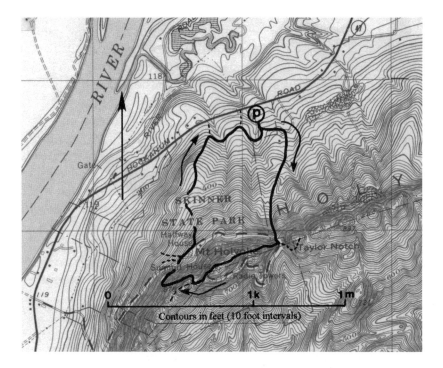

Contours in feet (10 foot intervals)

The Summit House

To continue the hike, find where the M-M Trail continues on the western side of the Summit House at the bottom of a flight of stairs. Follow the white markers past the road and parking area, and re-enter the woods. Not too far ahead, you will come to a trail junction in a small hollow. Bear to the right, leaving the M-M Trail, and follow the blue trail markers downhill. The trail descends to the Halfway House, steeply switching back on itself partway down. During winter, this dark and shaded section can be icy and dangerous. At the bottom, turn right onto the summit road, and then walk about 150 yards uphill, passing the Halfway House, to find a blue-marked trail coming in on the left. There is a sign here indicating that it is the Halfway House Trail. Turn onto this and continue your descent.

The Halfway House Trail is wide, easy to follow, and descends gradually through mixed hemlock and deciduous forest. At one point, it approaches Route 47, but then turns sharply right. From here, under cool hemlocks and tall white pines, the trail parallels Route 47, crosses a brook, and then skirts the rim of a second ravine. As the trail winds around the head of the ravine, keep to the left, staying with the blue markers. (If you bear right, you rejoin the Taylor Notch Trail which turns off here.) Your car is just ahead, downhill past the gate.

9

Mount Norwottuck

Rating: Moderate — relatively easy walking on wide paths with one very steep climb. Excellent views in all directions from the summit.
Distance: 4 miles
Hiking Time: 2.5 hours
Lowest Elevation: 525 feet;160 meters
Highest Elevation: 1,106 feet; 337 meters
USGS Quad: Mt. Holyoke (old series)
Other Maps: NEC Holyoke Range State Park - Eastern Section, ACC Amherst Trails, DEM map, NEOC Mt. Norwottuck, M-M Guide, Robert Frost Trail Guide.

Mt. Norwottuck is the highest peak in the Holyoke Range. It is one of the most popular hiking destinations in the Pioneer Valley, probably because of its commanding views of the countryside and distant hills. On a clear day, you can see Hartford to the south, Mt. Greylock to the northwest, and Mt. Monadnock to the north. A beacon tower was once located on the summit Mt. Norwottuck, built to guide aircraft taking off and landing at Westover Air Force Base. Also on this hike are the famed "horse caves" where local tax rebel Daniel Shays was said to have hidden during his rebellion in the years following the War for Independence.

The starting point for this hike is the Notch Visitor Center which houses a number of educational and informative displays about the Holyoke Range and its wild inhabitants. Maps can also be obtained here. Although the parking area is large, it can fill up quickly on a beautiful weekend, making this a good choice for a midweek hike.

One other note: Just below and north of the parking area is a shooting range. It is possible that the first portion of your hike will be disturbed by the sounds of gunfire. The combination of gunshots and the low pass of a C-5A transport plane from Westover Air Force Base will remind you that you have not really left civilization to enter this otherwise unspoiled area.

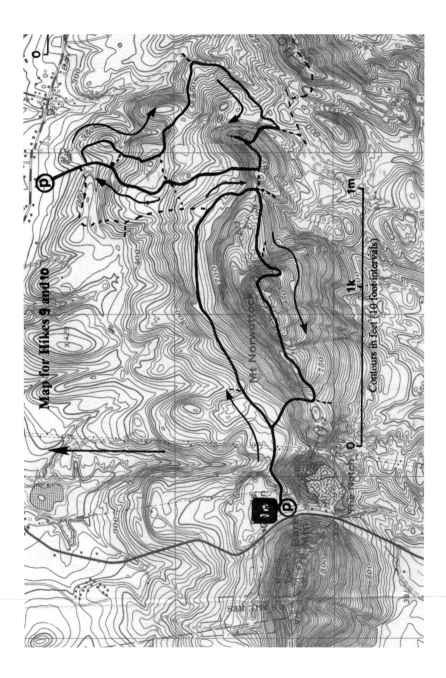

Map for Hikes 9 and 10

Mt Norwottock

Bare Mtn

The Notch

Contours in feet (10 foot intervals)

Trailhead: The Notch Visitor Center is located in the middle of a pass (called the "Notch") in the Holyoke Range, between Amherst and South Hadley. Massachusetts Route 116 utilizes this natural gap in the range, following the original Indian trail. Not long ago, a trolley line used it also. The highly visible parking area is found on the eastern side of Rte. 116 at the height-of-land, just north of the quarry.

Directions: Basically, this hike follows the Robert Frost Trail (orange markers) east to just below the summit, and from there follows the Metacomet-Monadnock Trail (white markers) west for both the climb and the return trip. These two trails run concurrently for the first and last half mile of the hike.

From the parking area, climb the stairs that lead to the Visitor Center (if open, restrooms and water are available). Follow the pavement ahead, swinging to the right, to the trailhead directory. The Robert Frost Trail (marked in orange) actually begins here and travels 40 miles north to Wendell State Forest. The Metacomet-Monadnock Trail (white markers) passes through here as well, and the two share the route for the first half mile. A third trail, the Laurel Loop, begins here also and is marked with blue tags on trees.

From this trailhead, follow the three overlapping trails east through a hardwood forest, then downhill through hemlocks, to the junction with the old trolley bed. Pay attention here! You will need to make a left, then a right, a left, and a right — all within a few hundred feet! After these turns, you will be on a gravel road heading east, following white markers. The next junction is met in a large power-line cut. Keep to the left, and enter the woods for good now, following the white and orange markers. In just a few hundred feet, the trails split at a fork. Keep left again, now following only the orange markers of the Robert Frost Trail.

After bearing right at another fork and crossing a small brook, the trail begins to climb, but only gradually and intermittently. There has been gypsy moth damage along sections of this trail. The overstory foliage has been periodically wiped out by these insects who seem to come in waves of destruction every eleven years. Tree trunks may reveal the tan egg clusters of the moths, and during outbreak years the

80

defoliation of the oaks keeps the trail well-lit, even bright, during the summer. After hiking 1.5 miles from the starting point, you will come to a junction with a well-used woods road coming up from Bay Road. Turn right here, still following orange markers, and begin a steep climb that leads to a junction with the M-M Trail. To the left, the Robert Frost and M-M Trails head east toward Rattlesnake Knob. If you have time, it is only a quarter mile walk to a nice overlook (see *Hike #10)*. But to stay on this hike, continue ahead, now following only the white markers of the M-M Trail. Pass the red-blazed "Swamp Trail" on the left.

The M-M Trail will soon swing to the left through an oak forest with an understory of mountain laurel and sheep laurel. At about 2 miles from the start of the hike, you come to a small stream crossing below the hanging ledges of the Horse Caves that supposedly sheltered the tax rebel Daniel Shays and his men. As you climb to the ledges, you will see that they are composed of sandstone and conglomerate, not the typical igneous basalt of the Holyoke Range. In ancient times, successive lava flows were interrupted by periods of sedimentary deposits. Look for an unmarked path to the right that follows the bedding plane. If you follow it for about 100 yards, you will come to some interesting arch-like formations that reveal the effects of water erosion, possibly during the glacial melt. Return to the M-M Trail and scramble up a jumble of boulders through a cleft in the cliffs. Pass a junction with a blue trail, and continue ahead and uphill on a rock-strewn footpath, following the white markers.

The next quarter mile is the toughest of the hike, and it can be a real challenge, requiring proper footwear in winter. As the trail climbs steadily to the summit, you climb over boulders and alongside small cliffs. Just before the last steep stretch, you pass a vernal pond and then a lovely and usually private overlook to the east. At the summit, where a beacon tower once stood, there are several overlooks to the north.

The views from the several overlooks along the perimeter of the summit are some of the best in the Pioneer Valley. From an overlook on the eastern side of the summit you can see the flashing lights of Westover Air Force Base, the bulk of Long Mountain, and the Pelham hills. Below you and due east is Rattlesnake Knob. From the northern overlook you can see Mt. Greylock in the distant northwest, with its long, flat southern plateau and its summit bump with monument. Further to the north are Vermont's Haystack and Mt. Snow where the reflection from the ski trails is visible in winter and early spring. Just behind the UMass buildings are the two Sugarloafs, and to the right, the mass of Mt. Toby. The white speck to the right of Mt. Toby is the Buddhist Peace Pagoda in the Leverett Hills. From here all the way to the southeast, the horizon is dominated by the walls of the valley. Only distant Mt. Monadnock towers above them in the north as does a bit of Wachusett Mountain in the east.

From the summit, find the white markers of the M-M Trail, and begin your 1.5-mile walk back to the Notch. This section of the hike, which is mostly downhill with a few little rises, is heavily used and shows wear. A partial overlook to the north is found on the right, partway down. At the end of the descent, you will come to the junction with the Robert Frost Trail that you passed earlier. Make a left here and head back to the Notch, following both white and orange markers. Remember to keep to the right when you cross the power-line opening, and pay attention to the several turns near the trolley-line junction.

Mt. Norwottuck

10

Rattlesnake Knob

Rating: Easy to moderate — a loop around the knob to its cliffs, with excellent vistas to the east and northwest.
Hiking Time: 1.5 hours
Distance: 2 miles
Lowest Elevation: 315 feet; 96 meters
Highest Elevation: 813 feet; 248 meters
USGS Quad: Mt. Holyoke/Belchertown (old series)
Other Maps: NEC Holyoke Range State Park - Eastern Section, DEM map, ACC Amherst Trails, NEOC Mt. Norwottuck, M-M Guide, Robert Frost Trail Guide

Rattlesnake Knob, located in the Holyoke Range, is the smaller peak just east of Mt. Norwottuck. Both peaks share the same general form, in that they rise steeply on the east and slope more gently to the west; both also have cliffs on their eastern faces. A series of north-south-trending faults along the Holyoke Range are responsible for the abrupt eastern faces of these two peaks, as well as the rather spectacular profile of what would normally have been a long, flat-topped ridge. This faulting, which pushed up deeper layers of lava in the eastern part of the range, is also the reason why the Holyoke Range runs east and west, not north and south as do all the other basalt ridges in the Pioneer Valley.

As for the name "Rattlesnake Knob," legend has it that Amherst College freshmen were sent to this peak to catch rattlesnakes as part of a nineteenth-century initiation rite. However, no rattlesnakes can be found there today. Much of the hike described below is within the Holyoke Range Conservation Area of the Town of Amherst. A series of trails located within this conservation area traverse the wooded north slope of the range and invite exploration.

For this hike, use the map for Hike #9 on page 79

Trailhead: The trailhead is located on the south side of Bay Road in Amherst, 1.3 miles east of the junction of Bay Road and MA Route 116 (which is at Atkins Farms, 4.5 miles south of Amherst center). There is an Amherst Conservation Commission sign locating the site, and parking for about 3 or 4 cars. Be careful not to block the gate to the service road, and please respect the privacy of nearby neighbors.

Directions: From the parking area, walk through the gate, following what was once an old paved road (Sanderson Lane) into the woods. Today, this is the service road to an Amherst water supply tank. You will see a few blue markers on trees, indicating that you are on the Ken Cuddeback Trail, which is the southern end of one of Amherst's longer trails. On the left, you will pass a backyard with a small pond, and just after a small rise you will pass a woods road marked with yellow markers coming in from the right. Continue ahead as the lane becomes a bit steeper. Look carefully for an unmarked footpath on the left, located about where the service lane begins to curve to the right. Near this trailhead you may find yellow markers, but the trail itself is unmarked. Following it will take you over a small brook and then immediately to another unmarked trail. Turn right on this unmarked trail and follow it south and uphill over a beautiful knoll of white pines with an understory of mayflowers. You will soon arrive at a junction where you cross over the small wooden bridge over the very small brook. (The trail to the right takes you up the knoll and down to the water tank — making possible a very short side loop.)

After crossing the bridge, the trail, now marked with yellow dots, rises through a hemlock woods, arriving in a few minutes at a swampy junction. It may be difficult to see the trails here, especially in spring when the ground is wet. Straight ahead are the yellow markers, but you want to bear left onto another trail, marked occasionally with red equestrian tags This trail heads uphill for a short distance but then levels out. It next skirts a wet area, which is often a mess caused by mountain bike usage, and then heads downhill to a junction with yet another unmarked trail, this one more of a lane. Turn right here and head uphill again.

The lane climbs steadily uphill through an oak forest, and just after a few turns, it comes to a marked trail junction located between a dark hemlock woods and the steep side of Rattlesnake Knob. Turn right here, now following white and orange markers. The climb is quite steep but not very long. At the top of the rise, turn right, and follow the blue markers 200 feet north along this ridge top to a viewpoint looking over a very steep drop. The view from this ledge takes in all of Long Mountain and the forest surrounding it. Another viewpoint is just ahead on the trail, on the left, and this one is aimed at the cliffs of Mt. Norwottuck, the Valley farm fields, and even Vermont's Mount Snow in the far distance.

After taking in the view, retrace your steps back to the junction, but keep to the right and stay on the ridge, now following orange, white, and blue markers. At the bottom of a short descent, make a right turn following the blue markers of the Ken Cuddeback trail. Then, almost immediately, this footpath begins a steep descent down the side of the mountain. Eventually the trail levels out and passes a red trail on the left. Not far past this junction, you should come to a wet area where the blue trail swings to the left (yellow markers continue straight ahead to the junction you were at earlier). The trail here is level for a short distance, but then it descends gradually through a mixed forest that includes some big white pines. Finally, just past a junction with a trail coming in on the left, the path drops down along the side of a massive water tank, which looks like an alien spacecraft, and meets the service road. From here, walk down the service road to your car.

View of Long Mountain from Rattlesnake Knob

11

Long Mountain

Rating: Moderate — a climb, steep in places, to a summit with a west-facing vista, and a long, gradual descent around the north side of the mountain where there are some wet areas.
Distance: 3 miles
Hiking Time: 2 hours
Lowest Elevation: 385 feet; 117 meters
Highest Elevation: 920 feet; 281 meters
USGS Quad: Belchertown (old series)
Other Maps: NEC Holyoke Range State Park - Eastern Section, Amherst Conservation Land and Trails map, M-M Guide.

Long Mountain is the most eastern major summit of the Holyoke Range, and its name derives from its long, plateau-like summit. The climb from the east is very steep in sections (potentially difficult and even dangerous in winter), and you should be prepared to use your hands. Along the way, you'll notice some Robert Frost Trail mileage signs that are placed every half-mile. Long Mountain is isolated and does not receive as much use as the other peaks in the Holyoke Range.

Trailhead: From Atkins Corner (junction of Route 116 and Bay Road in South Amherst, north of the Notch), drive 2.9 miles east on Bay Road, and turn right onto Harris Mountain Road. At 0.5 mile ahead, the Metacomet-Monadnock Trail crosses this road, and parking is available on both sides of the road. There is a stone boundary marker here (Amherst-Granby). The starting point for this hike is on the western side of the road where there are markers for both the M-M Trail and the orange-blazed Robert Frost Trail.

Directions: Begin your hike by following the trail that has both white and orange markers, heading west. After a short level section, the trail swings to the left and begins to climb, approaching Long Mountain

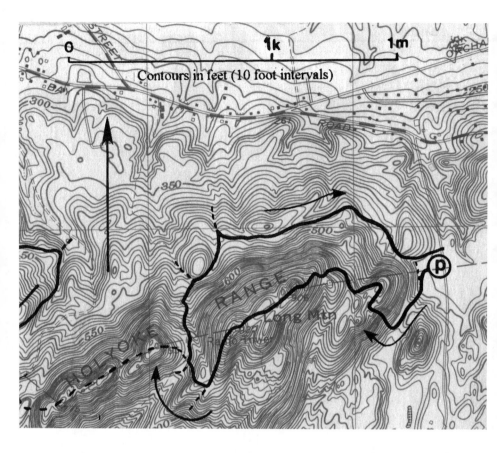

from the southeast. A recently built home that sits atop an isolated knoll is visible from the trail during winter. Ahead, where the trail begins a slight descent, look for a limited overlook just off-trail to the right. The trail continues downhill from here into a hemlock-filled hollow before it reaches the wall of the main summit. After a short detour to the right, the trail attacks the mountain. The climb is steep, but footing is aided by some log steps. After gaining substantial elevation, the trail leaves the hemlocks and enters a deciduous woods on a gradual slope that brings you to the eastern summit. Here, embedded in stone right next to the trail amongst hickory trees, you will find an old Amherst-Granby boundary marker. A sign nearby indicates that you are on "Hill 906," the unnamed eastern summit of Long Mountain.

From here the trail meanders up and down along the summit plateau, heading west. A few areas offer partial views to the north. One interesting feature of this summit is the vernal pond in a hollow to the left of the trail. The last uphill stretch brings you to the true summit of Long Mountain where the trail veers to the right and arrives at a fine overlook with Mt. Norwottuck dominating the scene. Nearby is the site of a former beacon tower, similar to ones that once stood on Mt. Norwottuck and Mt. Hitchcock. These were removed during the mid-1990s.

From the overlook, follow the markers down the hill on a footpath. At the bottom of the drop, the footpath joins a woods road onto which it turns right. Just ahead you will pass a junction with the Link Trail, and at the bottom of the descent, you come to a three-way junction. Bear to the right, heading north and following blue markers. After a short rise the trail will begin to descend through thick stands of mountain laurel. The course of the gradual descent is marked first by a hairpin turn, then by a long curve. Stay alert here and look for another three-way junction after this long curve, and then turn right onto a trail heading roughly east.

Follow this trail through a wet area, and keep your eyes open for yellow markers. After about 0.1 mile, you should come to yet another three-way junction. Bear right again here, almost doubling back on yourself, now following crude yellow and orange markers. After only 100 yards, turn left, off the lane and onto a footpath, still following the crude yellow and orange markers of an unofficial and non-maintained trail. You will now enter a beautiful hemlock woods and will cross some areas that may be wet during spring and after rains. Mountain bike use in recent years has resulted in the development of a second trail that is higher and more dry, running nearby and parallel to the main path (which is also used by snowmobiles). The trail follows a small meandering brook, then climbs a few feet up into a relatively dry forest. From here on, the trail winds its way east with some minor ups and downs. Where a lane comes in from the left, continue straight ahead. At the next junction, stay with the main trail which turns left and lead you directly to a gate and Harris Mountain Road. Turn right and walk back a hundred yards to your car.

88

12

Quabbin Park

Rating: Easy walking on roads and footpaths with one steep uphill stretch.
Distance: 3.5 miles
Hiking Time: 2 hours
Lowest Elevation: 524 feet; 160 meters (high water level)
Highest Elevation: 1,026 feet; 313 meters
USGS Quad: Windsor Dam
Other Maps: Quabbin Park Map (Friends of Quabbin, Inc.), NEC Quabbin Reservation Guide, NEOC Quabbin Park

Quabbin Park is the section of the Quabbin watershed that is located between MA Route 9 and the reservoir itself, near the Windsor Dam and Goodnough Dike. This is the best-known section of the Quabbin — and it is well-used. The visitor center is located here, as is the Enfield Lookout and the Quabbin Tower, a landmark on the summit of Quabbin Hill. A paved road traverses the general area, offering overlooks and parking at picnic areas. The Enfield overlook is frequently filled with cars, their owners scanning the horizon with costly optical equipment in search of bald eagles. The immense parking area just below the tower was built to handle huge weekend crowds and group visits. Since the attacks of 9-11 (2001), access to certain parts of the Quabbin, specifically the dams, has been limited. Hikers, like everyone else, are supposed to respect such barriers.

There is a quiet beauty to be found here along the many trails and old roads that cross the land of the Quabbin. The walking opportunities are excellent because of the number of old roads, many lined with foundations, and a good number of footpaths. The trail system in Quabbin Park is organized by numbered junctions and paint blazes on trees, and it invites exploration by extending into some remote areas.

Be sure to stop at the visitor center where you will find informative literature and maps, as well as interesting displays about the reservoir and its creation. The Friends of Quabbin, a non-profit organization, maintains the displays and sometimes even offers visitors coffee or tea. As explained at the beginning of this guide, the management of the Quabbin watershed is currently in flux. Prior to 2003, it was supervised by Boston's Metropolitan District Commission (MDC), but then the MDC joined with the Department of Environmental Management to form the Department of Conservation and Recreation, which now oversees the Quabbin.

Trailhead: The main entrance to Quabbin Park is located 3 miles east of the junction of MA Route 9 and US-202 in Belchertown. Pass the visitor center and then cross over the Winsor Dam. *(Note: At the time of this writing, access to the dam itself has been closed in response to heightened security concerns.)* Following signs to Goodnough Dike, drive around the spillway, through the rotary past the road to the tower, and past the Enfield Lookout. About 0.6 mile past the lookout, there is a parking and picnic area to your left. This area is called Hank's Place, a popular area that can fill up during peak use periods. (If it's crowded and no parking is available here, park at the tower and start the hike from there.)

A second route to Hank's Place is via the entrance to Quabbin Park, located on Route 9 about 3 miles east of the main entrance described above. Turning here and keeping left, and in about 2.3 miles, you will come to Hank's place, now on your right.

Directions: Begin by walking back to the main road on the lane that leads to the parking area. Cross the paved road and, still on the lane, enter the woods at marker post #24. *(Note: At the time of this writing, many of the marker posts were suffering from low maintenance. They may no longer be there.)* This is old Webster Road, one of the main routes to Enfield, an active village prior to the flooding of the Swift River Valley. To your left are interesting stone remnants of past life in this transformed area. After a short rise, you will pass what seems to be old cisterns located on both sides of the road. Just past these, look for a road leading off to the left (marker post 31). Don't turn on this

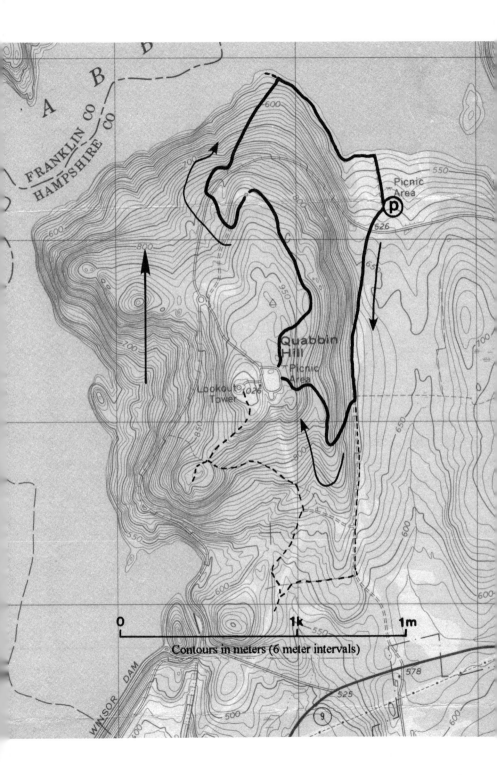

FRANKLIN CO
HAMPSHIRE CO

A B

600

700

550

Picnic
Area

P

526

800

600

950

700

650

Quabbin
Hill

Picnic
Area

Lookout
Tower

1026

650

850

900

700

600

550

600

550

0   1k   1m

Contours in meters (6 meter intervals)

WINSOR DAM

500

550

578

525

9

600

road, but walk on ahead just 50 feet or so to find marker #25 (on your right) and a footpath. Turn here, and begin a gradual climb to the tower. *(The hike can be extended from here. See text on **Extended Hike** at the end of this chapter.)

The trail to the Quabbin Hill is marked with yellow paint blazes on trees, as are other footpaths in Quabbin Park. After a swing to the left, the footpath passes through a pine forest and parallels Webster Road below it. It then switchbacks to the right and climbs more steeply before it reaches another level stretch. You have now reversed course and are heading north through a forest of oak, maple, hickory, and white birch. A final climb will bring you to the level of the parking area just below the tower. Yellow markers direct you to the right just before reaching the parking area. You may wish, however, to continue straight ahead on the well-worn path in the direction of the tower.

You have the option to visit the tower (it offers good views of the reservoir), then walk back towards the open cut (view) through the trees just to the right (north) of where you came out. You should find post #26 here in front of a picnic table. The trail markings may not be clear here, so walk toward the north end of the open cut, and bear right onto a yellow-marked trail. Don't walk down the well-worn path that heads downhill on the south side of the open cut.

Leaving the parking area, the yellow-marked trail snakes its way through a young, mixed-growth forest with an abundance of blueberry bushes as ground cover. It then heads gradually downhill, passing a large glacial erratic. After about 0.3 mile, you arrive at Wood's Place (named for its former owners) — a nice grassy area with four large white pines that offer rest and shade. A white garage is located here, the only standing remnant of the Wood family's former residence. To continue on, follow the lane that exits the upper (southwesterly) side of the clearing. At the first junction, make a right turn onto a lane that heads downhill, arriving at the paved road. This lane continues on the other side of the road, but you may wish to walk over to the Enfield Overlook, just to your right, for its view out to the Prescott Peninsula and beyond. Bald eagles that nest on the Prescott Peninsula are frequently sighted with telescopes and binoculars from this location.

Exploring old foundations on Webster Road

To continue the hike, return to the lane that crosses the road and heads downhill toward the reservoir. Some logging was done here in recent years. It passes under the Enfield Overlook and reaches the reservoir in about 0.4 mile. During wet periods, this lane can become very muddy. Just before you arrive at the water's edge, look for an unmarked footpath on your right, and follow it along the shoreline through a cool red pine forest. Spectacular views of the reservoir unfold as you walk. The large island to your left, with a peaked summit of 911 feet on its northern end, is Little Quabbin Island.

The footpath will swing around a cove that is frequented by waterfowl. Find your way across the cove (the trail is not clear), and arrive near a large white pine that stands at the edge of a clearing. Walk across the clearing, parallel to the shoreline, towards a small opening in a hedgerow. Cross over the small brook, and pass between two large maples, turn right, and walk up the lane (Webster Road) back to the parking area and your car.

*Extended Hike: (Note: This extension will add another two miles to your hike and is somewhat challenging in terms of trail-finding — but it is a very interesting route that will add even more variety to your hike. You may wish to use the Quabbin Park map and consult with someone at the visitor center about current trail conditions.)

Continue heading south on Webster Road past marker post #25. After another 0.4 mile, you will pass a lane off to the right. At about 1/8 mile further, turn right onto a second lane. (This one veers off just as Webster Road begins to descend and swing to the southeast.) This unmarked lane will lead generally west through a logged woods. Turn right onto a lane that enters a power-line cut, and look for trail markers that lead west and away from the power-lines. This is a wet area, and the trail heads west just before a pond. Once on this footpath, you should have no problems following it north along narrow ridges, past a large beaver pond, through dense forests, and eventually back up Quabbin Hill to the tower. From the tower, cross the parking area, and follow the directions above to finish the hike.

Tower on Quabbin Hill

13

West Quabbin Reservoir

Rating: Moderate — a walk downhill on abandoned roads alongside a brook to the Quabbin waters, and then back uphill.
Distance: 5.25 miles
Hiking Time: 3 hours
Lowest Elevation: 524 feet; 160 meters (high water)
Highest Elevation: 1,146 feet; 349 meters
USGS Quad: Shutesbury/Quabbin Reservoir
Other Maps: NEC Quabbin Reservation Guide

Before the Quabbin Reservoir was created, the roads that are utilized on this hike were main arteries from town to town, or farm lanes that connected homesteads. Today, the roads are dirt lanes, and only a few rock walls and foundations reveal former human habitation. This area also used to be a far more primitive and remote hiking area than Quabbin Park, the part of the reservoir that has been developed for public use. However, since the advent of the annual Quabbin deer hunt in the 1990s, the old paths have been upgraded to allow hunters to bring their vehicles closer to their prey. There is much wildlife here. It is not unusual to surprise a deer or to encounter a porcupine waddling down the trail ahead of you.

Trailhead: From the center of Amherst, drive east on Main Street which becomes Amherst-Pelham Road. An uphill drive of just under seven miles will bring you to the junction with US-202. Drive straight across this highway onto a gravel road that leads downhill to a small parking area at Quabbin Reservation gate #11.

Directions: From the parking area, walk back up to US-202, turn right (north) and walk along the highway for 0.5 mile, past a country store and gas station to gate #12. This gate is found at the end of a stretch of guard-rail. *Be careful here* — you are walking along a busy highway. (Note: While most of this road-walk can be done on the east side of the highway, you may wish to walk along its west side where the guard-rail limits the pathway).

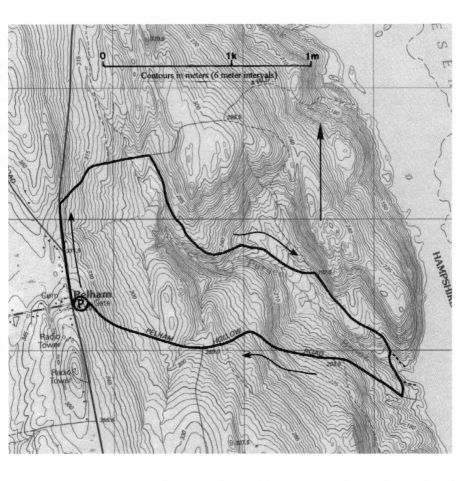

Walk around gate #12 and descend into the woods on the sand and gravel road. On your left is a cleared opening in the forest that is just below the overlook on US-202. As you walk, the sounds of the highway fade away behind you, and the scenery becomes more interesting. You will soon pass a small deer hunting checkpoint shed on the left. Further along, rock walls and clearings indicate the former presence of a farm. After about a half mile of walking, just after a stream crossing, the road forks at the bottom of a small valley. Turn right here and walk down a pine-lined lane where there is evidence of former beaver activity on the right. You will pass an area that was once dammed by these animals but where there is now a stand of ancient, and very dead, trees. Remnants of the dam and beaver lodge are visible also. This wetland is also where Purgee Brook begins.

96

From here, the woods road follows the north bank of Purgee Brook as it makes its way down to the reservoir. The walk-way is clear and easy to follow. Gradually, the vegetation changes from hardwoods to hemlock with a mountain laurel understory. Evidence of logging also becomes more apparent. After about 15 minutes of walking, you reach an open area where the trail and brook come closer to each other. Here, white pine becomes the predominant tree, with a ground cover of ferns below. On your left you pass the remains of a foundation of a house. Just a little past this site, you come to an open area where a sand bank rises high on the left. Here there is a lane on the left that leads in 0.2 mile down to the water's edge. If you decide to take this path to see the water, keep to the right at the first fork, and then return to this point to finish the hike.

Continuing on, the road heads more steeply downhill and then turns to the right. A section of this road is paved to prevent erosion. You cross Purgee Brook on a new bridge that, like the paved section of road, was built when the Quabbin Deer Hunt was established as an annual event. From here, continue on the road which follows the shoreline of a cove and passes under what was once a majestic stand of pine, but is now severely thinned from logging. Where the road swings to the right away from the water, look for a non-descript path (which may be blocked or hard to find) on the left. This path leads in an easterly direction along the cove's bank to some good viewpoints of the reservoir and the Prescott Peninsula. This is the easier of the two possible routes to the waters. Once you are on this path, it is easy to follow, and the woods are more open.

At the water's edge, you can sit on the pine needle carpet overlooking the reservoir. As you appreciate this "wilderness," keep in mind that on this very site there were once several homes, a public building, and not far way, a school. Later, if you're interested, you can identify these and other former building sites on an old map in the Pelham Historical Society's museum, which is located on the opposite side of US-202 from where you parked your car. The Historical Society's museum is often open on weekends during the summer.

After your time near the waters, return to the main trail (old Pelham Hollow Road), and begin the long trek back to your car. Although two roads come in from the left, stay on the main route which climbs uphill steadily between level stretches. The scenery along the way is mostly white pine, ferns, and rock walls that are reminders that years ago this was one of the major roads to the now abandoned and submerged town of Prescott. You will also notice that some logging has occurred in this area in recent years.

Quabbin Shoreline

14

Swift River Reservation

Rating: Easy to Moderate. Some trail-finding challenges.
Distance: 2 miles
Hiking Time: 2 hours
Lowest Elevation: 650 feet, 198 meters
Highest Elevation: 1040 feet, 317 meters
USGS Quad: Petersham
Other Maps: Trustees of Reservations

The Trustees of Reservations are the caretakers of three conservation areas located near Petersham on the east side of the Quabbin Reservoir. These are the Brooks Woodland Preserve, the North Common Meadow, and the Swift River Reservation. All three, as well as nearby Harvard Forest, preserve extensive woodlands which receive relatively few visitors and offer exceptional opportunities for walking and studying nature in relatively undisturbed conditions. When visiting the area, be sure to visit the Fisher Museum at Harvard Forest, located on Route 32 north of Petersham. At this museum, a series of beautiful dioramas tell the story of land use in this area and New England in general. The knowledge gained here will make your hiking experiences in the forests more interesting. Harvard Forest also has a number of trails that are noted on their trail map.

In this region east of the Quabbin, hikers will find quiet trails that are closed to motorized vehicles. Throughout these preserves, there are many traces of bygone habitation, mostly in the form of rock walls and old foundations, especially at the Brooks Woodland Preserve located just to the east of Petersham center. The East Branch of the Swift River flows through each of these reservations, feeding the Quabbin Reservoir, which itself drains into the Connecticut River at Chicopee. Thus, although technically this hike is not located within the Pioneer Valley, it does lie within the drainage of one of the Connecticut River's tributaries.

Most of the 439-acre Swift River Reservation was acquired in 1983 by The Trustees of Reservations. The reservation consists of three tracts, the largest being the Nichewaug Tract in which the hike described below is located. The Swift River flows through the center of this section of the reservation in a gorge. There is a vista overlooking this steep-sided gorge that will be passed on the hike described here. The river itself is a wild trout stream which is difficult to cross, so our hike will explore only one side of the reservation. Evidence of former and current farming is nearly everywhere in the form of old roads, rock walls, cellars, and cleared fields. The trails in the reservation are marked, but maintenance has been minimal. However, The Trustees of Reservations have produced a map of the area on which each intersection is designated by a number. At the time of this writing (2002), several junctions were not clearly marked, so hikers are advised to pay close attention to The Trustees map (if possible, acquire it beforehand), as well as the map and text below. Visiting the reservation several times will pay off in terms of route finding, and there are also many other trails and roads to explore.

Trailhead: From the junction of Routes 202 and 122 south of Orange, drive 7.8 miles south on Route 122 to its junction with Route 32 North. Turn right here on South Street, drive 1 mile and turn right on Nichewag Street. A small parking area for the reservation is located about 0.6 mile ahead on the left overlooking a large field.

Directions: Begin hiking from the parking area, heading south through a gate on a grassy lane that is normally kept mowed. Be alert for ticks and poison ivy in this section of the hike. The lane traverses a large field, with plenty of milkweed and other common wild field plants. At the end of this field crossing, the path enters the woods. The trail, now a rocky footpath, is denoted by circular yellow markings. You will pass near some cliffs to your left, and then enter a hemlock woods. At a fork, take the left turn, which, like other junctions and trails in the reservation, is not well marked. The trail will take you down to an open vista overlooking the gorge of the Swift River. This is the best vista on the hike, so be sure to spend some time sitting on the rocks and enjoying it.

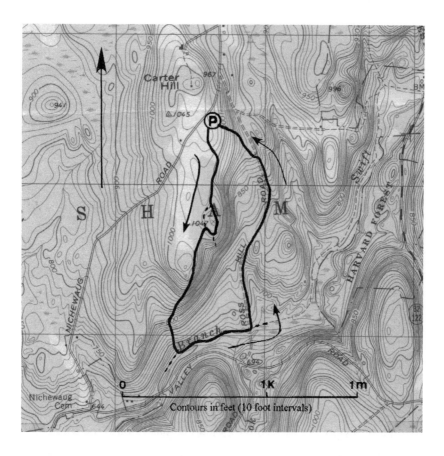

Contours in feet (10 foot intervals)

Continuing on, the trail passes a few lesser views on the left, and then descends further, passing what is marked on the map as junction 90. At this junction, keep right and follow the path uphill to junction 91. As of 2002, this junction was not well-marked, so you may need to pay very close attention here. At junction 91, you want to make a left turn onto another footpath on your way uphill. There is a rectangular yellow marker on a tree at the beginning of this lightly used and lightly marked footpath. (If you miss this turn and keep going, the trail heads north. *If you are pressed for time, you could head back to your car this way.*).

However, assuming you have correctly turned left at this junction (91), you will next have to scramble up rocks and then cross over old stone walls near a field. Here, the trail continues heading south and re-enters the dark hemlock woods — but not for long. Soon the lighting is brighter, and you find yourself in an oak forest with a low bush blueberry understory, and you are descending slowly along the edge of the ridge. Again, pay close attention to the pathway, and be very alert for a sharp left turn — do not continue to follow the trail ahead which passes through a grassy area as it heads downhill. (*You really need to make this turn. If you come to a wet area, you have missed it.*) So make that important left turn (there was a marker here in 2002), and begin to walk in a more easterly direction.

Making sure that you are following the sporadic yellow markers, push ahead through the overgrown pathway. The trail descends through a mixture of hemlocks and then passes to the left of a large boulder. Now you may begin to hear the sounds of the Swift River, and you pass under some monster hemlocks as you approach the waters. When you reach the river, turn left onto a path paralleling the river, now heading north on a well-defined path. Along the way, you will pass the remains of a dam and through some muddy areas aggravated by mountain bicycles. There are occasional yellow markers along the way, but you will not need them. In about a quarter mile, you will come to a raised bed where a road once crossed the river. Turn left here and follow this old road (Ross Hill Road) in a westerly direction. (At this point, you may wish to walk 200 yards straight ahead on the river path to view an active beaver dam that has flooded the trail.)

Ross Hill Road will take you past many rock walls. You will pass a lane on the left and a clearing at Clarks' Cellar hole, the remains of a former habitation. The walking is gradually uphill now, and the road is lined with old maples, obviously having once been a well-used passage over the river. You pass junction 92 (a footpath here leads uphill to the vista), and at junction 86 a trail goes off to the right. But stay on the main road, still going uphill, until you come to junction 85, which will be on the left. This junction is located near a point on the lane where a monster maple is embedded in the wall. On the opposite side of the road is a boulder field.

From this junction, follow the footpath west through a beautiful forest of white pines. In sections, the trail is covered with pine-needles, and the forest floor is green with ferns. The trail becomes steeper towards its terminus and then emerges at the northeast end of the parking area.

15

Mount Lincoln

Rating: Easy to moderate — an uphill climb on a footpath with some wet areas and brook crossings. Part of the hike is on forestry roads.
Distance: 3.5 miles
Hiking Time: 2.5 hours
Lowest Elevation: 600 feet; 183 meters
Highest Elevation: 1,240 feet; 378 meters
USGS Quad: Belchertown/Shutesbury
(Note: Some trails not accurately shown)
Other Maps: M-M Trail Guide. Cadwell Memorial Forest map (available near trailheads)

Mt. Lincoln is the name of a high point in the Pelham Hills that is crowned with several man-made towers. Like Mt. Tom (*Hike #7*), its height (1,240 feet) makes it an ideal location for radio and microwave transmissions, and today the summit of Mt. Lincoln might be best described as an antenna farm. A fire tower also stands tall on its summit, offering unique views of the surrounding terrain. You need not be discouraged by this technology, however, for the hike to the summit is interesting in itself. You will climb through a glen with several waterfalls, walk through a rich and varied forest, and pass a very old graveyard hidden in the woods. In recent years, however, occasional illegal ATV use has compromised the condition of several wood lanes in Cadwell Forest. You can also expect to encounter mountain bikes in this forest.

Nearly all of this hike is within the boundaries of the Cadwell Memorial Forest, which is owned and managed by the Department of Natural Resources Management, University of Massachusetts. The forest was a gift from the widow of Frank A. Cadwell, donated in 1951. Cadwell was a self-made businessman who made his start in the lumber business, but ended up as the president of the Amherst Savings Bank. He bought the land during a time when the mountain was no longer being farmed and land prices were cheap (about $5 per acre), and he eventually accumulated a block of about 1,300 acres. In the late 1940s, Cadwell's widow was unable to find a buyer for the land, even at $3 per acre, and so she gave it to the University. The forest currently occupies 1,195 acres and abuts some Amherst watershed land, creating a fairly large tract of woodland that is relatively undisturbed, with the exception of a few research and demonstration projects set up by UMass forestry students.

Trailhead: From the center of Amherst, drive east on Main Street (which becomes Amherst-Pelham Road) for 4.3 miles. Just past the Hawley Reservoir which is on the right, park on the left (north) side of the road. The Metacomet-Monadnock Trail crosses the road here, and there is space for about three or four cars.

Directions: Heading south, cross the road and follow the white markers of the M-M Trail into the woods. The trail in this section is within the boundaries of the Amherst Watershed. Just after a brook crossing on planks, the M-M Trail makes a sharp left, leaving the lane, and then crosses a seasonal stream bed. From here, the trail begins to climb, swinging left and then right, arriving at the bottom of a long, hemlock-shrouded ravine or glen. In this vicinity, you can see the remains of a old dam used for water power. From here, the trail follows the brook uphill, crossing it several times.

The glen is quite beautiful in places, with its several waterfalls and twisting stream. During times of high water, however, some of the crossings can be difficult. You will need to follow the white markers carefully as they will guide you along the best route through this sometimes challenging environment. Near the top of the glen the forest is brighter and better lit. This section of the forest was thinned in early 1989. The largest and most scenic falls are found here, just before the trail leaves the glen and meets a forest road called Cowles Lane. Turn left onto the road, leaving the M-M Trail, and follow it uphill in a southeasterly direction. After about 0.2 mile, bear right at a fork where the road, now more level, swings around to the right. This road is called Rich Street. At this point, an extension of the hike is possible and is described below.*

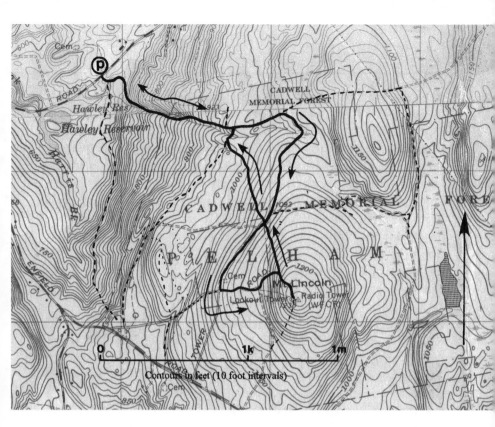

Contours in feet (10 foot intervals)

Continuing on, you will pass a few acres that are in the early stages of re-growth, and soon afterwards pass a road heading off to the left. You are now on Cemetery Drive. The forest in this section of the hike is quite varied and includes white birch, beech, several kinds of oak, hickory, and white pine. The understory is mountain laurel and sheep laurel, along with numerous ground plants and ferns. You pass the point where the M-M Trail crosses this road and continue walking until you come to a gate and another road junction. Turn left here onto Tower Road.

Just 50 feet after this left turn, there is a lane on the left that leads to a small, very old, yet well-maintained cemetery. This privately-owned cemetery is referred to as the Cowl's Lot. The 27th and 35th Massachusetts Infantry are represented here, though most of the other gravestones are too worn to reveal details. To continue the hike, return to the lane, turn left, and begin the uphill walk to the summit area.

The winding gravel road, which becomes paved near the summit, leads to the actual summit of Mt. Lincoln. You can also get there by following the utility lines, but this route is steeper and overgrown in recent years. At the summit you come upon modern communications technology, a maintenance building, and a fire tower. While there are some views of the valley through the utility line cut and the road, the best views are, of course, from the fire tower. To the south is Knight's Pond, and to the southwest you see distant Hartford and Springfield. A striking view of the Holyoke Range is to the right of these cities. To the northwest is Mt. Orient, and further away, the Sugarloafs and Mt. Toby, while Mt. Monadnock rises high above the northern horizon. A tiny piece of the Quabbin Reservoir, along with the Quabbin Tower itself, are visible to the southeast.

Leave the summit, and head back down Tower Road. Just ahead, where the paved road makes a sharp left, the M-M Trail bears right (north) near a medium-sized white oak. Turn here and follow the footpath into the woods. In about 0.25 mile, the trail will cross Cemetery Drive, enter a white birch-dominated woods, and then begin a descent. A wet area is traversed on bridges, and after that a small brook is crossed. When you reach the gravel road, turn right and walk only 100 feet or so to the point you were at earlier. A left turn here, still following white markers, will lead you back down the glen, back and forth across the brook, and eventually back to Amherst-Pelham Road and your car.

* **Extended Hike:** This will add about one more mile to the hike. Do not turn onto Rich Street. Keep left at this junction, and stay on Cowles Lane which continues uphill and crests just before it crosses high voltage lines. Turn right after (and below) the power-lines onto King Street, and follow this lane back under the lines. After passing some old rock walls, you should again turn right onto a lane, Middle Row, that now heads west. You will walk through deep pines, along some cliffs, and (keeping right at a junction) eventually arrive at the junction of Rich Street and Cemetery Drive. See map for details.

Waterfall on Mt. Lincoln

16

Buffum Falls

Rating: An easy and pleasant walk through hemlock forests and alongside running waters.
Distance: 1.0 miles
Hiking Time: under 1 hour
Lowest Elevation: 400 feet; 122 meters
Highest Elevation: 580 feet; 177 meters
USGS Quad: Shutesbury
Other Maps: M-M Trail Guide, ACC Trails Map

Protected as watershed land by the Pelham Conservation Commission and the Town of Amherst, this area makes for pleasant and relatively easy walking. Most of the hike is routed through a hemlock forest that surrounds and lines the ravines of Buffum and Amethyst Brooks. These evergreen trees make for cooler hiking during the summer. The waterfalls here are popular during hot weather, with visitors wading in the shallow pools, but these are the times when insect populations are most active. The woods here also support a variety of mushrooms that are found in abundance during late August and September.

There are a number of trails in this area that offer variations on the route described below. Some are not marked clearly, and some are not marked at all. Since 1994, several relocations of the Metacomet-Monadnock Trail were made. In 2000 the Amherst Water Department declared their reservoir off limits to hikers. Because of this, the hike described below differs from earlier editions of this book.

Trailhead: From downtown Amherst, take Main Street east about one mile to the traffic lights where it crosses North East Street. Continue straight through, travelling another 1.7 miles (the road is now called Pelham Road), and turn left onto North Valley Road. This turn is just under a mile past the Amethyst Brook Conservation area (on the left). At 0.5 mile from this turn, park at the parking area on

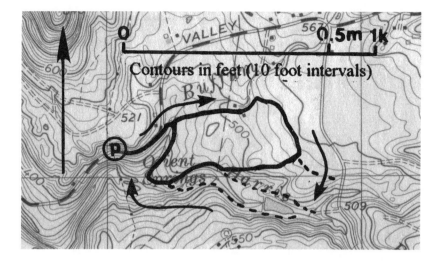

Contours in feet (10 foot intervals)

the left side of North Valley Road under the power-lines. There are spaces for several cars. The trailhead is about 400 feet ahead (north), on the right side of the road. (Note: Additional trail relocations are planned. It is expected that the new M-M Trail will be re-routed so as to cross North Valley Road close to this parking area. However, this hike is best started by following the directions below.)

Directions: After walking north along the road (*Be watchful of cars!*), the conservation area entrance is on the right, opposite the first house on your left. Follow the path down to the wooden bridge where you will find the white markers of the Metacomet-Monadnock Trail. Cross the bridge and head straight ahead on a lane following blue markers into a hemlock and pine forest.

Where the trail comes to a fork, keep left and closer to Buffum Brook. A short distance ahead, the trail enters an area that only ten years ago was completely open and dotted with plantings of juniper. By 2002 the maples had grown tall and their shade is now killing the juniper and other sun-loving plants that used to thrive here. Past this area, the trail swings closer to Buffum Brook and then arrives at a stone wall (and a large maple tree) where you should bear right, keeping the wall and some backyards of private residences on your left (please respect private property). This section of the trail can be muddy during wet periods. As you enter a pine woods with very little ground cover, look for a junction with the white-blazed Metacomet-Monadnock Trail onto which you should turn right.

The M-M Trail will lead you under tall pines through a high and dry area. After passing through a rock wall and descending to cross a small brook and a woods road, the trail comes to the edge of a ravine high above Amethyst Brook. Just ahead, follow the white markers of the M-M Trail to the left as they veer off the footpath. Take care on this steep descent on a narrow path that will bring you to the banks of Amethyst Brook. Here, in the dense hemlocks of the ravine, is a particularly remote section of trail with access to the brook. Follow the white markers of the trail downstream, but be ready for a turn where the trail climbs steeply out of the ravine and rejoins the blue footpath. A left turn here will bring you to the vicinity of Buffum Falls where there is a tiny clearing and a path down to the falls. This is an area worth exploring. If you go just a little further ahead on unmarked trails, you will find the confluence of Buffum and Amethyst Brooks.

From Buffum Falls, now follow the white markers of the M-M Trail north alongside Buffum Brook, passing several other waterfalls. You will soon arrive at the bridge that you crossed at the beginning of the hike. Turn left here, walk out to the road, turn left, and walk back to your car. (Note: other trail relocations are planned for this area in the future. It is possible that the M-M Trail will cross Buffum Brook just above the falls, switchback up the side of the ravine, and emerge very close to the parking area. This will eliminate most of the road walk.)

Buffum Falls

17

Mount Orient

Rating: Moderately challenging — a walk utilizing a series of marked and unmarked paths and a woods road, with significant elevation gain. There are also some brook crossings and wet, muddy areas.
Distance: 4 miles
Hiking Time: 3 hours
Lowest Elevation: 197 feet; 60 meters
Highest Elevation: 957 feet; 292 meters
USGS Quad: Shutesbury
Other Maps: ACC map, M-M Trail Guide, Robert Frost Trail Guide

This hike traverses a beautiful tract of land in southwest Pelham and eastern Amherst that is currently used for logging. Criss-crossed with woods roads, footpaths, and a power-line cut, it attracts hikers, cross-country skiers, and mountain bikers. Portions of the area are rugged and make for challenging hiking, yet other sections are perfect for easy walks. Three major brooks flow through this undeveloped (so far) natural area close to the town of Amherst. They join together to form the Fort River near the junction of Pelham Road and North East Street. Perhaps what is most remarkable about this well-used area is that little of it is publicly owned. Except for the Town of Amherst's 40-acre Amethyst Brook Conservation Area and Pelham's Mt. Orient Conservation Area, it is private interests, including developers and lumber companies, who own the rest. This hike is rated "moderately challenging" in part due to its elevation gain, but more so because half of it is on unmarked trail (as of this writing). Numerous intersections may be confusing and will require close attention to the text and maps. But don't let this discourage you, the scenery will repay the effort.

Trailhead: From Main Street in the center of Amherst, drive one mile east to the junction with North East Street and then straight ahead (through the traffic lights) on Pelham Road for 0.8 mile. The paved parking area of the Amethyst Brook Conservation Area is on the left, and there is room for about 20 cars to park. The trailhead is in the center of the parking area, just beyond a few boulders.

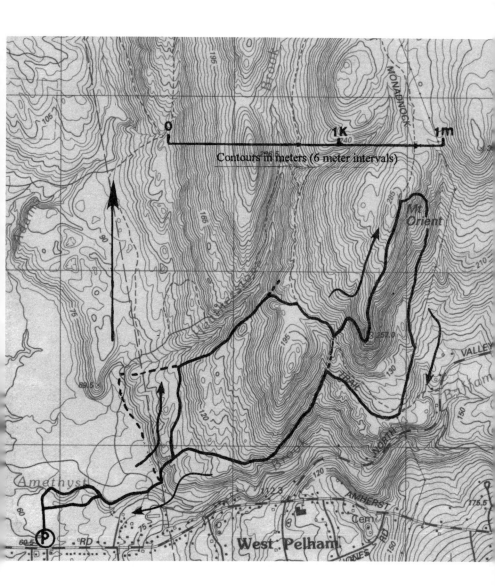

Contours in meters (6 meter intervals)

Directions: From the trailhead go north, following the worn path, passing working fields, and some that are returning to nature. You are walking on part of the 40-mile long, orange-blazed Robert Frost Trail. Watch for canine droppings, as this is a favorite dog-walking area. When you come to a wide open field, keep to the left, following the narrow path towards a small opening in the woods. (The Robert Frost

Trail turns to the right here.) Soon you will find yourself on a trail marked with yellow markers, and you will cross Amethyst Brook on a wooden hiker's bridge. Now follow the yellow (with red or orange dot) markers onto a path that will swing around in 0.1 mile and meet the brook again, crossing a small tributary on rocks or on a small log bridge. The trail now follows along the north side of Amethyst Brook and will lead you to a second bridge — don't cross it. You are now back on the Robert Frost Trail (RFT) and should see orange markers. (*Crossing the bridge here and following the directions in the last paragraph is a short-hike option that is very suitable for small children*).

At the bridge, bear left following the path alongside the brook, passing a third bridge (don't cross it) where the trail veers away from the brook. Next, still following the orange RFT markers, follow the trail as it crosses a logging road and approaches the steep sides of the mountain; the chassis of an old car rests nearby. The trail swings to the left here and proceeds uphill. Next, where the trail turns right, look for an unmarked trail going up and off to the left of the trail that heads in a westerly direction. Follow this unmarked, though easy-to-follow trail through a grove of stately hemlocks, up and around small knolls, eventually arriving at a real car junkyard. Slowly decaying bodies of mechanical behemoths of the past will greet you here near a junction with another unmarked woods road.

Turn right onto this non-maintained woods road, which is used by snowmobiles and all-terrain vehicles (ATVs), and follow it uphill. As it is abused, drainage is a problem in many places. Expect mud and water. A stream is below you to the left, and you may hear it running in the spring. After 10 or 15 minutes of walking you should arrive at what was once a small clearing (there are some small white birches here, the first trees to colonize open forest). Note that the trail forks just ahead — turn right here. This trail rises through the woods, "slabbing the slide" of the hill (hiking on a steep angle). The trail then swings to the left and meets a large and potentially very wet lane that is also frequented by ATVs. Turn right here, and navigate the many wet spots, all of which have alternate routes where you can keep your feet dry.

In just a few minutes of walking, you will arrive at a junction with the Robert Frost Trail. This junction can be recognized by the profusion of markers on nearby trees — the double yellow markers of the Amherst Conservation Commission, the white markers of the M-M Trail, and the orange markers of the RFT. Turn left here, and head north over a rocky outcrop and up a steep slope. Where the trail reaches the cliffs, you come to a narrow opening between a rock and a tree, with a drop-off to the right, but don't panic. There are two ways to proceed from here. You can go left and scramble up the rocks and out to the ledges, following the orange and white markers. An alternate approach that is more gradual is to continue straight ahead on the now unmarked footpath which swings to the left and up. This path is not always easy to follow, and it deteriorates into several footpaths towards the end, but if you follow it uphill, keeping to the left, it brings you to the ledges in no time at all.

Regardless of which route you take, you will soon find yourself on the eastern crest of the protruding ridge of Mt. Orient, which offers one of the best viewpoints in the Valley. From these gneiss ledges, you see the entire Holyoke Range, from Long Mountain to Mt. Holyoke, extending along the southern horizon. In the foreground are the heavily forested lower flanks of the mountain, and beyond them the fields and houses of Pelham and Amherst. The flatness of the rocks from this vantage point, and of course the extensive view, makes this an excellent place for a rest and refreshment.

To continue the hike, walk north and uphill on the RFT and M-M Trail over slabs of gneiss to what appears to the summit of Mt. Orient (it is not). A small campsite is located here. Turn left here, and follow the trail downhill through dark hemlocks, then up again to the west side of the mountain where you may catch a nice breeze. The trail next rises to a wooded, relatively narrow ridge top which it follows for some distance. Be aware that the trail is still gently rising and soon passes the nondescript and unmarked summit of Mt. Orient. After a slight descent, look for a junction with an unmarked trail on the right. This junction is marked with a cairn (small pile of rocks). Take this trail to the right and follow it first to the north, then down the eastern side of the mountain in a forest of hemlock and mountain laurel. As you descend, the trail becomes wider, crosses a small stream, and in about a half mile arrives at a power-line cut. Turn right here, entering a completely different environment, which is unnatural in some ways but offers with much more light.

After following the path along the power-line cut for a few minutes, you will come to a 5-way junction — continue straight ahead here, do not turn left or right, and continue keeping the woods to your right. Next, you will drop down to a lane in front of pole #34146, where you should turn right and enter the woods. You are now back on the white-marked M-M Trail, hiking on a level and wide lane that passes through a mixed deciduous forest. In just a few minutes you will see or hear a waterfall in the woods on your left (more so in spring or after heavy rains), and then you arrive at a junction with the RFT. Turn left here, and begin following only orange and yellow markers. The trail now begins a long descent on a rocky lane. Keep right at the bottom of the decline, and continue to follow the orange markers downhill. There may be a few wet areas on the way down, but for the most part, this is an easy and pleasant walk through hemlock woods. You can expect to encounter mountain bikers in this section. After about 25 minutes, you will arrive at the bottom of the mountain near the lone car wreck that you passed earlier.

Continue straight ahead and follow the orange markers across the woods lane and then back to the brook and the bridge. Don't cross this bridge; instead, turn right and follow alongside the brook until you reach the second bridge. Cross here and then bear right, following a path (there are some yellow markers here) that is parallel to Amethyst Brook, though some distance away from it. You will soon arrive at the clearing and pass some gardens where the path swings to the left and leads back to your car.

Bridge over Amethyst Brook

18

Fitzgerald Lake Conservation Area

Rating: Easy to Moderate, depending on trailhead. Some pleasant woods walking with a few ups and downs, out to a small lake in a wilderness setting — all in Northampton!
Distance: 3 miles
Hiking Time: 2.5 hours
Lowest Elevation: 190 feet, 58 meters
Highest Elevation: 330 feet, 101 meters
USGS Quad: Easthampton 7.5' x 15'
Other Maps: Fitzgerald Lake Conservation Area map

Fitzgerald Lake was created in the mid-1960s to be the focus of a future housing development. The project had to be discontinued when protections for wetlands became stricter during the 1970s. The land comprising Fitzgerald Lake Conservation Area began to be acquired by the City of Northampton in 1977 and is now about 500 acres in extent. Fitzgerald Lake itself, named for the family who owned the property, is about 1/2 mile in length and is completely surrounded by forest and wetlands. The conservation area is co-managed by the Broad Brook Coalition, a non-profit conservation organization, and the Northampton Conservation Commission. There are three access points to the trail system near the lake that are described on the Fitzgerald Lake Conservation Area trail map and brochure. Note: Much of this hike can be very wet, as well as rocky; be sure to wear appropriate footwear.

Trailhead: From the junction of Damon Road and Routes 5 and 10 in Northampton, drive north on Routes 5 and 10 for 1.3 miles. Turn left onto Coles Meadow Road. This turn is just past North King Motel and across from the State Police Headquarters. Drive 0.1 mile and turn left on Marion Street, and drive 0.2 mile to the end of the street where there is a wide patch of pavement where two or three cars may be parked. Do not proceed up the unmarked lane because it is the

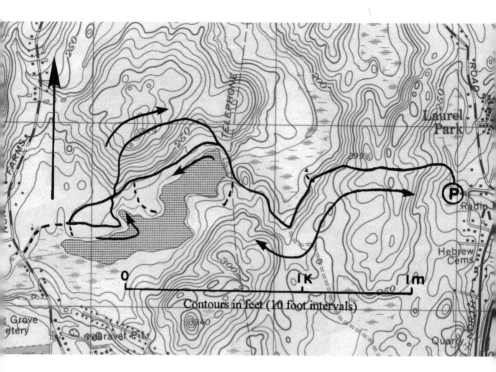

Contours in feet (10 foot intervals)

entrance to a private residence. Blue markers will be found on the north side of this pavement designating the start of a trail. Just 50 feet ahead on this trail is an information post for the Fitzgerald Lake Conservation Area. This is clearly a residential area, so please respect the rights of residents and the neighborhood near this trailhead. Park your car thoughtfully, being careful not to block driveways, and make no disturbing noises.

Directions: Follow the blue markers of the Marian Street Trail, passing the map box and a residence on your right. The newly-cut trail first climbs up and around some rock outcrops and then comes to a large boulder near a trail junction. A white-blazed trail comes in here on the right. Keep to the left, and continue following blue markers. The cut trail soon joins an established woods road and passes through stands of mountain laurel. At the next junction, bear right — there is a sign directing you to "Fitz Lake" posted here. The trail now begins to drop in elevation, and after passing under dark hemlocks, you will arrive at a junction in a low, wet area where boardwalks lead to the right and left. For a short side excursion to a wonderful nature spot, go to the right, and in about 100 meters or more, there is a wildlife blind overlooking a marsh called Cooke's Pasture. This open area is full of birds and wildlife, and the blind is raised above it, offering a stunning view of the magical surroundings.

To continue the hike, retrace your steps back to the boardwalk junction, where you now take the left turn. Follow the blue markers as the trail climbs out of the swampy area and onto more dry land. You soon arrive at a junction with a woods road, the Boggy Meadow Road. Turn right here, and walk through the pine forest to the southern end of the dam that makes Fitzgerald Lake possible.

Proceed to the northernmost part of the dam, and follow a short footpath in the open field that leads west to the shoreline of the lake. It may be wet in places here. The path will lead immediately to a trail junction — keep to the left here, following the Lake Trail. This trail follows the northwestern side of the lake, although it is a ways from the actual shoreline. This trail is very rocky and riddled with tree roots — watch your step! Small boardwalks take you over the wettest areas.

Where the trail climbs a few feet above the low-lying lake shore, you enter an environment that includes a variety of ecosystems. Here are dry oak forests next to wetter hemlock stands, big boulder outcrops, and some very wet areas. (Take notice of a trail, the Narrows Trail, that leads off to the left to a secluded part of the lake's shoreline. You may wish to explore it.) Continue following the Lake Trail up and over a gentle rise. You pass a junction with the red Hillside Trail (which will be part of your return route), and you cross over a small brook. You are now in a section of the conservation area that has numbered posts designating natural features of interest. Pass by a boulder (post # 10), and continue straight ahead over a small rise and through a hemlock woods to a trail junction.

A right turn at this junction will bring you to a raised bridge over a wet area and then to a boardwalk on your left that leads to the water's edge. Boats are launched from here. In this vicinity there is information about the numbered natural features along the trail. Further ahead, on pavement, is the North Farms Road trailhead.

But to continue the hike, turn left onto the Fishing Place Trail, marked with white markers. Hemlock and white pines are the dominant trees in this section of the forest. You pass a man-made debris shelter on your left, made from dead branches. Soon the lake becomes visible. Continue ahead on the pine needle-covered path to a point of land facing the open lake. A beaver lodge is to the left near the opposite bank. Ironwood trees, a tangle of vines, and wild rose bushes are found at this point.

Continue further along the Fishing Place Trail, which now reverses direction, following the edge of a small arm of the lake. Before the dam was built, this arm was merely the drainage of small stream. Boardwalks lead you over wet areas. You pass a fallen tree with its entire root system exposed, and then arrive at the trail junction you passed earlier, near the large boulder. You have just completed the first short loop of this hike. Cross the small brook that feeds the arm of the lake that you have just walked along. A community of swamp species grow here, including skunk cabbage, ferns, and red trillium. Cross the brook on planks, and in another 50 feet you arrive at the trail junction you crossed earlier. Turn left here, now following the red markers of the Hillside Trail.

The Hillside trail is much rockier than the trails you have been on so far. At first it leads through a wet area, sometimes on boardwalk, but then it begins to climb into a much drier area of the forest. In this section, oaks begin to predominate, although there are still some hemlocks and some small white pines. Mountain laurel crowds the path, and some club mosses can be seen among the limited ground cover. As the trail climbs out of the swampy lowlands near the lake, the footing becomes rockier, and the prominent features are large boulders and outcrops of only one rock type, gneiss. At several points you pass through some very thick stands of laurel, which blooms in late June. As the trail begins to descend, notice the hardwood forest around you. There are at least three kinds of oak growing here — white oak, red oak, and black oak — along with sugar maple and some sweet birch.

121

The trail continues to descend and gradually approaches the level of the lake, passing through another wetland traversed by boardwalks. You arrive at a trail junction that you passed earlier, not far from the lake. Make a left here, and follow the unmarked path, which may be wet, out to the grassy dam. Walk across the dam and enter the woods again on Boggy Meadow Road, following it to the Marion Street Trail, where you should turn left. Follow the blue markers on your way back to the parking area (pay close attention at the many junctions, most of which are marked with signs).

Cattails on Fitzgerald Lake

19

D.A.R. State Forest

Rating: Moderate — a long walk on woodland footpaths, up to a fire tower and back down to a lake.
Distance: 5 miles
Hiking Time: 3.5 hours
Lowest Elevation: 1,417 feet; 432 meters
Highest Elevation: 1,697 feet; 517 meters
USGS Quad: Goshen
Other Maps: DEM Map

Located on the western edge of the Pioneer Valley, D.A.R. State Forest is best known as a camping and swimming recreation area. Within its acreage, however, are about 14 miles of foot trails, mountain bike trails, bridle trails, and gravel or dirt roads. Outside of the heavily used Upper Highland Lake area, the forest offers solitude, an environment of beautiful hemlock woods, a strangely balanced boulder, and the wilderness view from the fire tower on Moore's Hill, the forest's highest point. At 1,697 feet, this is the highest elevation of any hike in this guidebook.

The D.A.R. State Forest was created in 1929 as a gift to the Commonwealth from the Massachusetts Daughters of the American Revolution, and it has the distinction of being the first D.A.R. forest in the United States. From an original tract of 1,020 acres, the forest has grown to its present size of 1,536 acres. During the 1930s, the Civilian Conservation Corps lived and worked in the forest, repairing dams and building many of the forest roads now used as hiking and bridle paths. A number of the buildings in the forest, now used for recreational and administrative purposes, were built by and housed these C.C.C. workers.

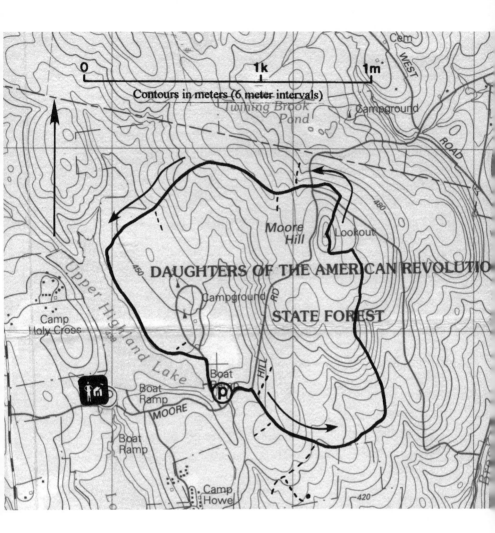

The trail marking system in the forest is the official DEM trail marking system, in which all hiking trails are marked with blue triangles, hiking-bridle trails with red, and winter use trails with orange. The markings are not entirely consistent in this forest, and many markers have been removed or have fallen off trees. More recently, the New England Mountain Bike Association (NEMBA) has done some trail work in the forest, and some trails now have plastic markers indicating the names of the trails or their destination. NEMBA has also built a few boardwalks over wet areas.

Trailhead: The most direct way to reach the forest from the Northampton area is to follow MA-Route 9 (Berkshire Trail) for 15 miles to Goshen, and turn right (north) onto MA-Route 112. Less than one mile from this turn off of Route 9 is the well-marked entrance to the D.A.R. forest. During the summer season (Memorial Day to Labor Day) a fee is charged for parking and day use ($5 in 2002). From the ranger's office and toll booth area, drive 0.5 mile ahead, following signs for the campsites and boat ramp. Turn left through a gate, and park in the lot to the right.

If you wish to avoid the parking fee, one option is to continue driving north on Route 112, and then go east on Route 116. From South Ashfield, turn off of Route 116 and follow the paved Williamsburg Road, going south for about 3 miles. Turn right onto Ludwig Road which will take you to the D.A.R.'s eastern boundary and a gate. Park your car on the side of the road, follow the road uphill for 1/4 mile, and start the hike with paragraph #6 below. While you are on Williamsburg Road, you will pass Chapelbrook Reservation, owned by The Trustees of Reservations, with its inviting waterfalls and ledges — another place certainly worth exploring.

Directions: From the parking area, walk back on the paved road to Moore Hill Road (the main road you came in on) and turn left. Follow the road up a slight rise for about 0.2 mile. Just after a curve in the road, you will find a trailhead on the right. Turn right onto this multi-use trail which is marked sporadically with both red and blue markers. Soon, you will pass a mountain bike trail on your left that leads directly to the fire tower. Continue straight ahead, and soon you will pass another trail (the Sunset Trail) coming in from the right. In the spring, this is a good area for finding forest wildflowers such as pink lady's slipper or painted trillium. Continue ahead as the trail winds around a small rocky ridge (with its own glacial erratic), and then down to a junction with a trail that still retains some old orange markers.

If you would like to view an unusual sight in this otherwise typical hardwood and hemlock forest, the following are directions for a side-trip that takes about 20 minutes. (If not, skip to the next paragraph.)

American Toad

Turn right at this junction to follow the orange-marked trail for about 0.2 mile, and make a left turn onto a blue-marked trail. This junction occurs just before the orange trail makes a dip into a small ravine. In about 0.1 mile, the blue trail will lead to Balancing Rock, a gigantic boulder precariously perched on an exposed slab of bedrock. It was left in this position by the retreating glacier during a previous ice age. After viewing the monolith, retrace your steps back to where you began this side-trip.

If you did not take the side-trip, turn left at the junction with the orange-marked trail. If you took the side-trip and have returned to this junction, continue straight ahead, heading more or less east, on the red trail. After a gradual downhill, a small brook crossing, and another short rise, the trail passes through a long stretch of remote hemlock woods before it dips slightly to cross another, larger brook. After crossing this brook, which is at an elevation of about 1400 feet and is

126

the lowest point of the hike, the trail is heading north and begins to rise toward the summit of Moore's Hill, a climb of about 300 feet. (Be alert in this section as the markings are sporadic, and the trail often braids to accommodate horses on wetter ground and mountain bikes on drier ground.) Fortunately, the most difficult portion of the climb is finished quickly, and the rest is very gradual. Notice the shiny pieces of mica in the rocks in this section (the rock is mica schist). After a long walk at a mostly steady elevation, you come to a gravel and sand road on which you will turn left, heading uphill. The road will swing to the right, passing through a spruce grove, ending at the fire tower on the height of land called Moore's Hill, elevation 1,697 feet.

Unless you happen to be hiking on a cloudy or hazy day, this fire tower won't disappoint you. There are views of forest and mountain for as far as you can see, and you can experience a wind that you hadn't realized was blowing. To the southeast are the Holyoke and Mt. Tom ranges, to the west is Mt. Greylock, and to the northeast you will see the Chapelbrook ledges and distant Mt. Monadnock.

To continue the hike, *do not* take the trail to the left (northwest) of the fire tower that follows the utility lines. Instead, take the trail directly in back (northeast) of the fire tower. This trail quickly swings to the right and is marked sporadically in blue. Cross the dirt road, and continue downhill on the footpath as it swings to the west. After less than 0.1 mile, you will come to paved Moore Hill Road.

Cross the paved road, and re-enter the woods on the "Long Trail," the name given to this footpath marked with blue markers. You will immediately cross over a very small brook and enter a rocky area through hemlocks. Large chunks of quartz are visible in the exposed bedrock that the trail utilizes in places, as well as in nearby boulders. After a descent over rocks and through a forest of hemlock and birch, the trail crosses a small, wet area that can be muddy. After a short level stretch, a descent, and a walk through a dark hemlock grove, the trail follows a series of boardwalks built by NEMBA that traverse a wet area. The spring wildflowers here include violets and marsh marigold. At the end of this short section there is a trail junction. The trail to your left leads to the campgrounds. Continue straight ahead on the Long Trail.

The trail now passes through another hemlock woods. A swamp and then a stream will be on your right. Finally, you arrive at the north shore of Upper Highland Lake, which was created about 150 years ago to provide daily surges of water to power mills in Williamsburg. The Long Trail now swings to the left and heads south along the shoreline in a hemlock and white pine woods. Views of the water are blocked by clumps of mountain laurel along the path. You see another trail which swings away from the shoreline and heads to the campground, but you continue ahead along the shoreline to the camper's beach. After crossing the beach, follow the gravel road for a short distance away from the lake, and turn right onto a trail that will lead in about 0.1 mile to the paved campground road and the boat launch area. The parking area and your car are just ahead on the left.

Upper Highland Lake

20

South Sugarloaf

Rating: Easy or difficult, depending on conditions — a walk through woods with some extremely steep sections that are easy to navigate in summer but can be dangerous in winter or during very wet times.
Distance: 1.5 miles
Hiking Time: 1.5 hours
Lowest Elevation: 190 feet; 58 meters
Highest Elevation: 652 feet; 199 meters
USGS Quad: Mt. Toby
Other Maps: NEC Mt. Toby Trail Map, Pocumtuck Ridge Trail Map

Although the mileage and elevation gain of this hike are on the low side, the steepness of the trail in two sections makes this hike potentially dangerous under certain conditions. Hikers are advised to exercise extreme caution on the steep sections near the cliffs when the ground is wet, and to wear cramp-ons under icy conditions.

South Sugarloaf mountain is located in South Deerfield, just over the Connecticut River bridge (MA-Route 116) from Sunderland. Like North Sugarloaf, the larger hill to the north, as well as Mt. Toby, it is composed of hardened coarse sediments that have resisted river erosion. The far-reaching views from South Sugarloaf's summit and steep ledges inspired the construction of a summit house in the 19th century. Following acquisition by the State, this house was replaced by an observation building and picnic pavilion. While most visitors to this well-placed summit drive up in cars, hikers will get more of a work-out and will also encounter more private overlooks.

Trailhead: On MA-Route 116, drive 0.5 mile west of the Sunderland bridge, turn north (right) on Sugarloaf Street, and park in the sandy parking lot 100 feet to the right, just past the entrance to the summit road. This unmarked parking area that can accommodate many cars.

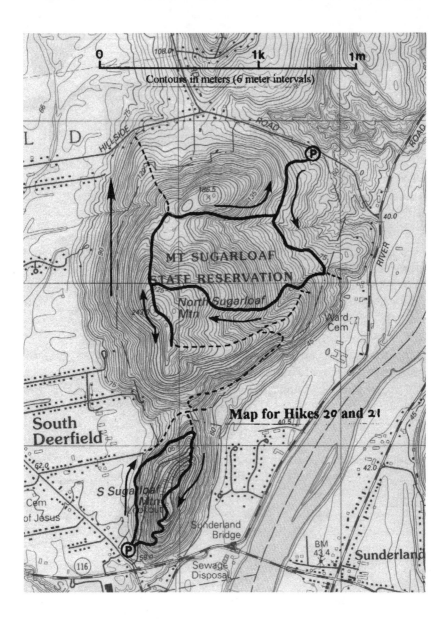

Contours in meters (6 meter intervals)

Map for Hikes 20 and 21

Directions: From the south end of the parking area, enter the woods following a lane that approaches the summit road but then swings left (north). From here, near a utility building, the lane (now marked with red markers) parallels a utility line cut that heads northeast along the west side of the mountain. This is the West Side Trail.

After a walk through hardwoods, the West Side Trail turns right just before a farmer's field. Ahead, the trail crosses the power-line cut, swings up and around to the left, finally joining old Mountain Road, on which it turns right and begins to climb. The rocky summit and cliffs of North Sugarloaf may be visible through the trees to your left. At the Y-junction, follow the red markers to the right onto a narrow and eroded path that will lead in a short distance to a T-junction with the blue-blazed Pocumtuck Ridge Trail. Turn right, continuing the climb, now following blue markers.

Just before reaching the summit road, the trail scrambles steeply uphill to the left (on steps), reaching the guard rail. Follow the outer guard rail which will bring you back to the point where the trail re-enters the woods. The trail, now a footpath, winds and climbs steeply through laurel, hemlock, and maple along the eastern face of the mountain. The narrowness and steepness of this section requires great caution under slippery conditions. Be alert for a switchback where the trail abruptly swings right and then left. Just after this point, you reach a junction with more established trails.

There are three options at this junction. A right turn, through a tunnel of hemlocks, leads in about 200 feet to a view of North Sugarloaf. Straight ahead leads through woods to the parking area. However, to stay on this hike, turn left following the trail that parallels the summit's eastern escarpment. Blue markers are inconsistent here, so just follow the worn path, with its railroad tie steps, to pass two spectacular lookouts over cliffs with views of the Connecticut River, Sunderland, and Mt. Toby. Just after this vista, the trail reaches the lower parking area of the developed summit area. Follow the pavement uphill, past the upper parking area and the picnic pavilion, to the summit observation building.

This open summit offers one of the best views of the Pioneer Valley. To the east is the massive Mt. Toby, and the town of Sunderland is just across the river. To the south, the Connecticut River arcs gracefully toward the heart of the Holyoke range, a perspective that is frequently photographed. The gap between this range and the Mt. Tom range is clearly visible, marked by the tall stack of a power-generating station. Because of its accessibility, the South Sugarloaf summit is a popular place, and if you are hiking here during the tourist season, you won't be alone. During the summer, historical displays and photos of the old summit building can be seen near the stairways that lead to the observation tower. Just ahead on the hike is a more private and rugged place to enjoy the view.

At the south end of the summit you will find a trail (renovated in 2000) that leads steeply down the south face of the mountain. Originally, this trail was a series of well-terraced switchbacks to the summit, but later a utility line was cut through the center, and this unfortunately encouraged hikers to simply climb and descend in a straight line — a practice that increased erosion. Today, many of the switchbacks are preserved in the descent, but not all — in order to accommodate the continued growth of some endangered plant species which had grown undisturbed for many years previously.

Follow this newly renovated trail as it swings back and forth downhill via switchbacks and stairs. At the bottom of the descent, the trail turns to the right, leaving the power-line cut for good. In less than 100 yards you will reach the summit road again. Cross it, hop the guardrail, and walk back through the hemlocks and pines to your car.

The summit observation building on South Sugarloaf

21

North Sugarloaf

Rating: Easy to moderate — a woodland walk, partly on lightly maintained trail and wet in places, that climbs to steep cliffs with a fine view.
Distance: 3 miles
Hiking Time: 2 hours
Lowest Elevation: 240 feet; 73 meters
Highest Elevation: 791 feet; 241 meters
USGS Quad: Mt. Toby
Other Maps: NEC Mt. Toby Trail Map, Pocumtuck Ridge Trail map

To the immediate north of South Sugarloaf is a second, larger mass of conglomerate (Sugarloaf Arkose) called North Sugarloaf. Without a road to penetrate its wilderness or an observation tower to attract visitors, this mountain offers the hiker a quiet, private walk along small streams, a medium-sized summit swamp, and a striking view over cliffs to the west. South Sugarloaf and undeveloped North Sugarloaf are both administered by the DEM as the Mount Sugarloaf State Reservation.

There is an old Indian legend about the origin of the Sugarloafs and the Pocumtuck Range, which represent the petrified body of a huge beaver. According to Dr. Richard Little (*Dinosaurs, Dunes and Drifting Continents* (3rd edition), who relates this legend, a great beaver once lived in a great lake. The beaver had evidently offended Hobomuck, who decided to kill it with the trunk of an enormous oak. The tremendous blow split the beaver into different parts. His head became South Sugarloaf, his shoulders became North Sugarloaf, and his back turned into the Pocumtuck Range. It has been suggested that this legend tells the story of glacial Lake Hitchcock, which drained thousands of years ago, leaving great changes in the land formations.

For this hike, use map for hike #20 on page 130

Trailhead: From MA-Route 116 on the west side of the Sunderland Bridge, turn north on River Road in Deerfield, and travel along the east face of the two Sugarloafs for 1.5 miles. Turn left onto Hillside Road, and park at the gate and trailhead located 0.3 mile ahead on the left. There is parking here for about four cars.

Directions: Walk through the gate and enter the woods on a lane marked with red and blue blazes. This is the Hillside Trail and the (new) Pocumtuck Ridge Trail. After a short jog to the right, the trail turns left and heads deep into the woods away from the road. The moss-covered trail climbs gradually and then levels off somewhat before reaching a small brook, which may be dry in summer. The Hillside/Pocumtuck Ridge Trail turns right here, but continue straight ahead, crossing the brook and entering a trail marked with yellow blazes. This is the Brook Side Trail.

Although the Brook Side Trail begins on an old woods road, it soon narrows to a footpath. This trail does not get as much use as the other trails on North Sugarloaf, and it is in need of clearing in some places. After about 200 yards, it makes a sharp left, heading downhill. Be alert for a right turn; taking this will bring you through a few wet and muddy areas to a brook crossing. Here, during wet periods, the water cascades over small ledges. Just after this crossing, the markers show that you turn sharply right and then lead you up to a lane that parallels the southern side of this unnamed brook. You are now heading upstream with the brook on your right. After another 200 yards, the yellow-blazed Brook Side Trail meets another lane coming in from the left and then crosses the brook again. It now follows the brook uphill along its northern bank, passing a few small dancing cascades along the way. The walking in this section is relatively easy in spite of the uphill grade, and the trail is easy to follow in spite of the infrequent markings. After another half mile, the trail veers to the right, leaving the brook and climbing through laurel and hemlocks to the dry oak-dominated summit plateau of North Sugarloaf. From here, the yellow trail (now a small footpath) snakes its way through brush beneath the hundreds of dead oaks, the victims of the gypsy moth. After 0.5 mile, you will reach a T-intersection with the blue-blazed Pocumtuck Ridge Trail. Turn left here onto this wide, well-used path.

The Pocumtuck Ridge Trail follows the wooded summit rim of North Sugarloaf. The drop-off to the valley below, visible through the trees, is considerable. In about 0.2 mile, you will reach the great overlook. Below is South Deerfield and a row of old tobacco barns. Due west are the highlands that lead to the Berkshires. You may wish to explore further south along the ridge, where you will find a few viewpoints that look towards South Sugarloaf. After your visit to this part of the mountain, retrace your steps on the blue-marked trail, passing the junction with the yellow trail as you head downhill.

The blue markers of the Pocumtuck Ridge Trail will lead you steeply downhill, parallel to the western rim of the mountain. Just after crossing the runoff from a swamp on your right, a trail junction is reached. Turn right here, onto the red-and-blue-blazed PRT/Hillside Trail, and follow the winding footpath along the north edge of the summit swamp. As the trail heads downhill, it is joined by a brook on the right. There are potentially muddy sections here, depending on the season. In under 0.5 mile, the PRT/Hillside Trail turns left, away from the brook (at the junction with the yellow trail). From here, retrace your steps back to your car.

View of South Sugarloaf from North Sugarloaf

22

Pocumtuck Rock Loop

Rating: Easy to moderate — some climbing, some trail finding, and many good views.
Distance: 1.8 miles
Hiking Time: 1.5 hours
Lowest Elevation: 520 feet, 160 meters
Highest Elevation: 852 feet, 260 meters
USGS Quad: Greenfield
Other Maps: NEC Pocumtuck Ridge Trail Map

This hike utilizes a new section of the Pocumtuck Ridge Trail (which traverses the two Sugarloafs), all of the Pocumtuck Range, and ends north of Poet's Seat Tower in Greenfield. Much of the trail is near or on land owned by the Eaglebrook School or Deerfield Academy, or on lanes with public access. Two ski areas are passed along the way — one currently operated by the Eaglebrook School; the other was abandoned long ago. (All that remains are a few structures, parts of a rope tow, and a great view to the east of Mount Toby.) Some of the trail sections are newly cut, and hikers are advised to pay close attention to markers.

Trailhead: From the junction of Routes 116, 5 and 10 (near exit 24 on I-91), drive 5.4 miles north on 5 and 10, and turn right onto Pine Nook Road. There are signs here for the Eaglebrook School, and this turn is across from Memorial Hall in Old Deerfield. Follow Pine Nook Road, climbing for one mile. On the way, you will go under a railroad bridge, pass by a number of Eaglebrook School buildings, and then the road's pavement will end. You arrive at a small, 3-car parking area on the right.

Directions: The first leg of this hike is from the parking area to a west-facing vista on the Pocumtuck ridge, which is locally known as Pocumtuck Rock. There are two ways to reach this overlook: by the unpaved service road or by a series of unmarked footpaths that parallel the service road. Either way, it takes 20-25 minutes to hike.

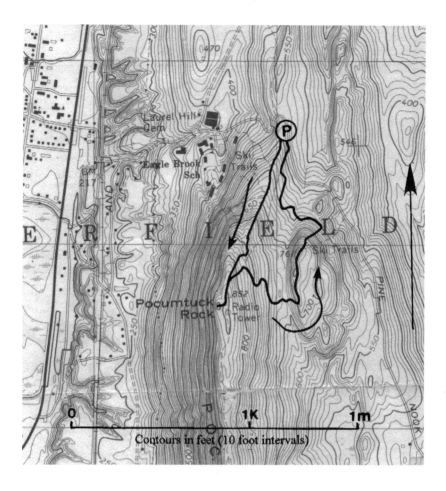

In order to take the service road route, leave the parking area and walk a few hundred feet ahead on Pine Nook Road. Turn right onto the service road, and follow it to the summit. At the beginning, and again near the top, you will see the blue markers of the Pocumtuck Ridge Trail. Do not follow the blue markers as they turn off the lane. On the way to the vista, you will pass the upper lift station of the Eaglebrook School ski area. Near the final part of the rise, the road splits — turn right to reach Pocumtuck Rock. There are also two communication towers and some utility buildings in this area.

The unmarked footpath option begins right at the parking area. These paths are shown on the topographic map, but what's on the map and what's on the ground are somewhat different. Leave the parking area, following the path uphill through clumps of mountain laurel. When you come to a lane, turn left, cross the gate, and walk over to the main service road and then turn right. Follow the service lane for a while and then walk toward the ski lift but turn sharply left before you reach it and follow this footpath to the top. Walk to your right towards the overlook.

The 180-degree vista from Pocumtuck Rock takes in the entire Deerfield Valley. The colonial town of Old Deerfield and the Deerfield River itself are clearly visible below you. Further to the northwest in Vermont is Mount Snow. The rock that composes the ledges you stand upon is a red conglomerate. Unfortunately, there is much evidence here of frequent visitations by careless hominids, no doubt due to the ease of access. You may find empty beer containers and other litter strewn around on this otherwise beautiful spot.

Leave the vista and return to the main service road, heading back downhill. Where the service road turns sharply left, go straight ahead, following blue markers on a newly cut trail. You pass through clumps of laurel and, at the bottom of the descent, cross a lane. Continue following the blue markers of the PRT. You pass over a slab of grey conglomerate and then over a raised road bed that carries you through a low lying area. Just past a small abandoned utility building made of concrete, the trail comes face to face with a basalt ridge that is parallel to the main Pocumtuck Range. After a short, steep climb under dark hemlocks and up a talus slope, be ready to make a left turn off the main trail. Now scramble up to the edge of the ridge amongst moss and blueberry bushes, and then follow the trail as it wanders off to the right down to an area of pines. The markers next lead to the left and up another small slope to the site of an abandoned upper skilift station, an old rope tow that was part of a long defunct Deerfield Academy ski area. From this place there are good views to the east, and if you leave the trail and walk in a westerly direction, you will find good views to the north as well. Anywhere in this vicinity makes a good spot for a rest. There are steep cliffs at the western edge of this small ridge, so be careful.

To continue the hike, follow the trail along the summit, straight across the old ski slope on moss and pine needles. The trail then descends the ridge steeply with switchbacks and arrives at a lane. Turn left here, following the blue PRT markers, but walk only for a short distance on this lane and be alert for a sharp right turn onto a newly cut footpath. This turn is marked but hard to find (it comes right after you pass two large hemlocks). The trail leads over a small drainage and then meanders through the woods. After a slight descent, the trail rises up to a junction with the service road to Pocumtuck Rock. Turn right, and walk down for 200 yards to Pine Nook Road, make a left, and return to your car.

View over Deerfield from Pocumtuck Rock

23

Mount Toby

Rating: Moderately strenuous — wet in places, with a steep climb to the summit.
Distance: 4.5 miles
Hiking Time: 3 hours
Lowest Elevation: 400 feet; 125 meters
Highest Elevation: 1,269 feet; 387 meters
USGS Quad: Mt. Toby/Greenfield
 (Note: Newer 7.5' X 15' map shows some trails inaccurately)
Other Maps: NEC Mt. Toby Trail Map, Robert Frost Trail Guide

Mount Toby is a massive natural feature located in the town of Sunderland. Standing taller than any other mountain in the Pioneer Valley (1,269 feet), Mount Toby offers hikers outstanding views, several waterfalls, and a good workout — an elevation gain of almost 900 feet. Located near a border fault (the valley of Route 63), Mount Toby is composed of a coarse conglomerate that was eroded from ancient mountains to the east. The resistance to weathering of this Mount Toby conglomerate has allowed it to remain poised high above the land around it. This conglomerate, a mixture of reddish-brown sand with pebbles of varying sizes, is visible in the many cliffs along its sides, most of them hidden by vegetation.

It is said that the mountain was named for Captain Elnathan Toby, who was reportedly the first settler to reach its summit. Its height has always made it a popular destination, and a hotel was built on its summit in the 19th century, as was done on Mount Holyoke, Mount Tom, and South Sugarloaf. It has long been used by students as a botanical and geological resource. In 1916, the Commonwealth acquired 755 acres and placed the land under the supervision of the University of Massachusetts. Since that time, the acreage has grown to nearly 1,500 acres, including parcels added by the Massachusetts DEM and Department of Fisheries and Wildlife. One tract acquired by the Commonwealth links the mountain to the Connecticut River.

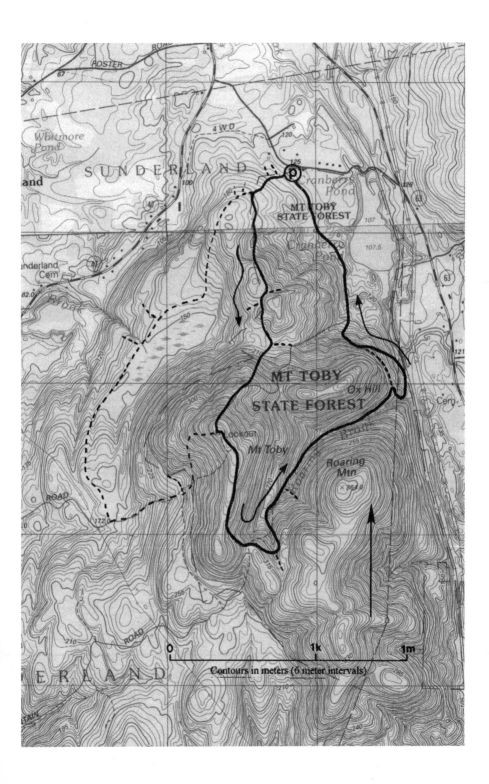

Trailhead: From Sunderland Center, drive four miles north on MA-Route 47, and turn right onto Reservation Road. In 0.5 mile, you will find the entrance to the Mount Toby Forest marked by a sign on your right. About 100 meters further ahead, park in the small parking area.

Directions: From the parking area, walk back to the Mount Toby Forest sign, pass through the gate, and make an immediate right turn onto the Robert Frost Trail (RFT), identified by its orange markers. This woods lane is also the route of the Sugar Farms Trail, named for its route through an area of maple sugar production, which is blazed with dark blue markers. *(Note: Previous editions of this guide used the Sugar Farms Trail to reach an eastern approach to the summit. This route has been abandoned in favor of using the RFT because the damage caused by ATVs in recent years has turned this lane into a continuous strip of muddy ruts.)*

The trail immediately begins to climb under hemlocks, passing two side trails coming in on the right. The climbing continues at a steady incline as the trail winds through the dark forest. Just after a sharp bend to the right, you come to a trail junction. Turn left here, leaving the lane you have been on, and follow the orange markers of the RFT uphill on a footpath. The climb is short but steep, leveling off near a clearing on the left. At a T-junction, turn right and follow the RFT as it winds around a rocky outcrop of Mount Toby conglomerate, drops a few feet, and then passes through a pine plantation, alongside green ferns, and over reddish-brown needles. The trail now swings to the left, crosses a wet area, and meets the Telephone Line Trail. This junction is marked by two red marks on a birch. Turn right here, heading uphill to the summit.

To reach the summit, you need to gain about 500 feet in elevation, so be prepared for an unrelenting climb. The Telephone Line Trail that you are now on follows the utility lines to the fire tower. It is an unnatural cut in the forest, but the exposure to light created by this cut allows many species of plants to thrive, including mountain laurel, blackberries and blueberries. The trail surface is mostly solid, but some sections may suffer from water erosion. Before reaching the summit, you will pass a trail coming in on the left, and for a short distance the trail slips back into the woods.

Mount Toby's summit makes an excellent spot for lunch or a rest — there is a clearing, a fire tower, a utility building, and some picnic tables. Formerly the site of a hotel, the summit clearing is grassy and pleasant. There are no views from the ground level, but the fire tower rises above the tall oaks that dominate the summit. The climb up the tower is exhilarating, and the views of the Holyoke Range, Mt. Greylock, and Mt. Monadnock are excellent.

The return leg of this hike is longer, but less steep. From the east side of the summit area, look for a lane marked with both orange (Robert Frost Trail) and blue markers; it swings immediately to the right heading downhill. Originally the carriage route to the hotel, this Summit Road is today the service road for the fire tower. The downhill walk here is pleasant, not too steep, and nearly always dry. As you descend further, Roaring Brook will come in on the left and run parallel to the lane. Beyond this point, the Robert Frost Trail leaves the lane, heading steeply uphill to the right on a footpath. Continue the descent following the Summit Road, now marked with white blazes, through a particularly scenic stretch of tumbling brooks.

Roaring Brook crosses under the lane three times during the next half mile or so. Just past the third crossing, where the brook drops down steeply and disappears below you on the right, and near where the Summit Road swings left, look carefully for a blue-blazed trail on your right. You have a choice here. The Summit Road will take you back to your car without any challenges other than distance. But for the adventurous, a detour on this side trail, named the Roaring Brook Trail, will make the hike more interesting. (*Warning - this trail is very steep and potentially dangerous, especially when wet or icy. Also, this trail can easily be missed as it does not meet the summit road at an obvious junction.*)

If you choose to do so, follow the Roaring Brook Trail steeply downhill, over huge rocks, and around the face of a cliff to a view of Roaring Brook Falls, the biggest waterfall of this brook; it is spectacular when water is abundant. From the falls, follow the blue markers down and out toward the railroad tracks. Just before reaching the tracks, turn left and follow an unmarked footpath (parallel to the tracks) through a grove of hemlocks for about 100 yards. Turn left onto a well-defined footpath, more or less continuing your northerly direction. A few orange and yellow markers denote this trail, which leads, after a gradual rise, back to the Summit Road. Turn right and follow the road, passing a junction with the Telephone Line Trail, back to the gate and parking area. *En route*, Cranberry Pond will be visible through the trees to your right.

Northwest vista from Mt. Toby

24

Rattlesnake Gutter and Vicinity

Rating: Moderate
Distance: 3 miles
Hiking Time: 2 hours
Lowest Elevation: 600 feet, 183 meters
Highest Elevation: 1016 feet, 310 meters
USGS Quad: Shutesbury (old series)
Other Maps: M-M Guide

Located in Leverett, Rattlesnake Gutter is a steep, narrow ravine with many rock outcrops on its northern edge. It is a significant natural feature, and it is being preserved by a local environmentally-minded citizen group, the Rattlesnake Gutter Trust. The place owes its name to the fact that rattlesnakes used to live on south-facing cliffs along Rattlesnake Gutter Road. Old newspaper accounts record that these snakes were driven to extinction for sport. During the 19th century, they were killed, probably by alpha male hominids (or at least wanna-be alpha males), and their rattles attached to belts as a personal trophy of sorts. A dirt road runs through the Gutter, which allows access to its entire length. This makes hiking it more of a stroll, but it is worth seeing. This road is closed during the winter months.

The hike described below takes you up into the hills surrounding the ravine, past the stone remains of an old mill site, and back to your car. You can then chose to walk past your car and take a look at Rattlesnake Gutter. For the very adventurous, there is an optional extension to the summit of Brushy Mountain; at 1,260 feet it is one of the higher points in the region. With the exception of Rattlesnake Gutter Road, the land traversed on this hike is privately owned. The owner, W.D. Cowls, has generously allowed outdoor recreationists, motorized and non-motorized, to use his land for day-use purposes. However, much of the Gutter itself is land trust property.

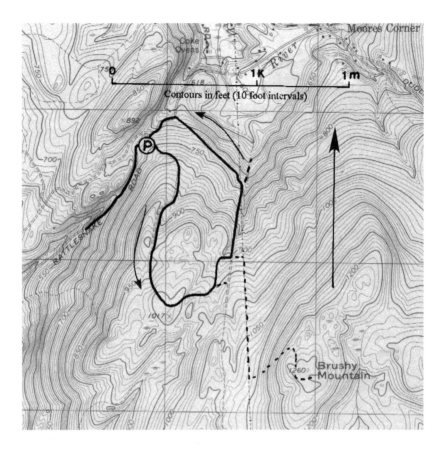

Trailhead: From North Amherst Center, drive 8.3 miles north on Route 63 to North Leverett Road. Turn right here — there are signs for Lake Wyola State Park. Drive another 3.8 miles to the Leverett Village Co-op store, and make a sharp right turn onto Rattlesnake Gutter Road. After another 0.3 mile, you pass a cemetery, and then in about 1/2 mile, you pass old Mill Yard Road. From here, the dirt road narrows and climbs. In just under a mile from the Co-op there is a small parking area on the left. The white markers of the Metacomet-Monadnock Trail should be visible nearby.

Directions: From the parking area, begin hiking south on the M-M Trail on a woods road. In places, the trail may be quite wet, but after a short climb the trail swings to the east and into a drier woods. The trail now rises and falls as it winds its way through the woods and then arrives at a junction where the marked M-M turns left onto a recently cut trail. Just after this junction you will begin to notice some rock walls, and soon you will arrive at the remains of an old mill. Passing over the small dam for the mill, you come to a junction with a prominent woods lane frequently used by ATVs and dirt bikes. To your left is the old route of the M-M Trail, which you will need to take in order to complete the loop and return to your car. To your right the M-M Trail continues heading north, leading in just a few minutes walking to the ruins of the Jonathan Glazier homestead which has been dated at 1790. Old stone walls parallel the road in this area. *(Straight ahead is a lane that leads out to a power-line cut. From there it is possible to climb to the summit of Brushy Mountain, which is completely wooded — See description below for Extended Hike.)*

Turning left at this junction, follow the lane north, crossing a brook. Immediately after this brook crossing, be alert for a fork — leave the dirt road you are on, and turn left onto a less-used lane. You may see the old markings of the M-M Trail along the way. During the spring and after rains, this section of trail may be wet in places. A brook has taken over portions of the trail route, which is what happens when a trail is not maintained. The trail will continue to lead downhill, eventually reaching a wide dirt road onto which you should turn left. This road will lead to Rattlesnake Gutter Road. Turn left again and walk uphill to your car.

From here, you may wish to walk west for about a half mile on Rattlesnake Gutter Road and explore the scenic ravine on your right. The rocky sides and giant boulders make this one of the more dramatic natural features in the region.

Extended Hike: From the junction near the old mill site, it is possible to reach the summit of Brushy Mountain, a wooded high point nearby. This requires some effort and careful attention to your surroundings. The entire route to Brushy Mountain is on unmarked paths or snowmobile trails, and it will add at least another mile to your hike.

Take the lane in front of you out to the power-line cut, and turn right. Next, go north on the dirt route under the high-voltage power-lines (used by ATVs and dirt bikes), passing several sets of double poles that support the power-lines. About 200 yards or more below and to the north of the height of land on the power-line cut is a point where (in 2002) two ATV lanes converge. One of the high voltage poles here is numbered 34087. Look for and follow a snowmobile trail which is on the east side of the power-line cut here. This trail enters the woods and begins a series of switchbacks as it climbs up the west side of Brushy Mountain. On the way, you pass a large glacial erratic. Near the actual summit, another snowmobile trail comes in from the right. The non-descript summit is reached just past a wooded swamp. The coordinates for the summit, posted there on a tree, are 42N28.32 and 72W25.96. Return to the old mill site by retracing your steps.

Coke oven near Rattlesnake Gutter

25

Wendell State Forest

Rating: Moderate — a downhill walk along cascading streams, then uphill to open cliffs looking north and west.
Distance: 3.5 miles
Hiking Time: 2.5 hours
Lowest Elevation: 689 feet; 210 meters
Highest Elevation: 1,182 feet; 360 meters
USGS Quad: Millers Falls
Other Maps: DEM Wendell State Forest Trail Map, M-M Trail Guide

Wendell State Forest, located north of Shutesbury and south-east of Millers Falls, is large (7,557 acres), remote, and wild. It is also the scene of many festivals and rallies during the summer season. The Metacomet-Monadnock Trail passes through it, the Robert Frost Trail terminates here, and a number of gravel roads penetrate the tract. The only "developed" section of the forest is near Ruggles Pond, where there is swimming and picnicking, and even this area is not heavily used. Free DEM maps of the forest are available from a case located near the parking area. This map shows the roads of the forest accurately, but does not do so well with the trails.

In addition to the 3.5-mile circuit hike described below, there is another possible hike of 1.5 miles that circles Ruggles Pond. At first, this trail follows the east shore of the pond, then moves away, passing through a very large stand of hemlocks. After crossing an open field and picnic area, it returns to the parking area. The full route takes about one hour to complete.

Trailhead: From Millers Falls, take Wendell Road east for 2 miles and turn right, following signs to Wendell State Forest. The forest headquarters and road to Ruggles Pond are 3 miles ahead on the left. From the headquarters, drive 0.2 mile to the pond, and park in the large parking area on the left. A parking fee is collected during the summer.

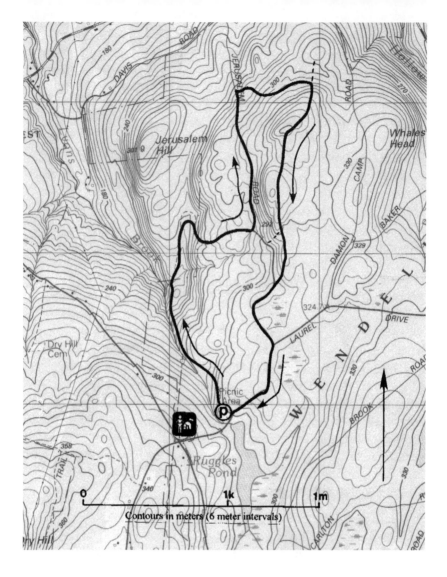

From Lake Wyola in Shutesbury, follow North Leverett Road east past the lake, make the sharp left turn and then turn left onto West Road which forks off about 0.4 mile ahead. West Road will lead to Montague Road in 2 miles; turn left here and drive 2 miles west to the Wendell State Forest headquarters and the turnoff to Ruggles Pond — both are on the right. Summer parking (fee collected) is at the parking area opposite Ruggles Pond, about 0.2 mile downhill from the headquarters. Off-season parking is at the forest headquarters.

150

Directions: The first section of this hike utilizes the white-blazed Metacomet-Monadnock Trail, which follows the road from Forest headquarters down to the pond, and then enters the woods at the far northern end of the parking area near some picnic tables. There is a large sign here indicating this trail. The trail quickly drops downhill from the parking area, soon passing an Adirondack camping shelter just before a brook crossing. Ferns, mountain laurel, and sheep laurel crowd the usually wet trail. As the trail continues descending, it moves closer to Lyons Brook, the runoff from Ruggles Pond, in the ravine to your left. Finally, at a convergence of brooks, the trail opens up and offers a view of several small waterfalls. Ahead, a third brook enters from the right, its water splashing over large boulders. After crossing this brook near its merger with Lyons Brook, the trail swings sharply right, leaving the rushing waters.

A short but steep climb brings you to a level section of trail that first crosses and then follows a small brook upstream. Next, the white markers of the M-M Trail turn right onto a woods road. This lane gains elevation steadily, making up for the descent along the brook, and passes through a forest of giant hemlocks, alongside a huge rock wall partially hidden by trees to your left. At a T-junction with a gravel road, make a left to leave the M-M Trail. This is Jerusalem Road. Walk about 0.4 mile, and turn right onto the Lookout Trail which is marked with blue tags. (This trailhead can easily be missed; it is about 0.1 mile past a tiny pond and parking space on the left hand side of the road.) The Lookout Trail climbs gradually to a ridge, and it joins the M-M Trail on the way (keep right). At a 3-way junction located in mountain laurel, turn right, and walk 100 feet to a magnificent overlook.

The view from this overlook normally takes in a 120-degree vista, but it has become obscured in recent years (this may change if the growth has been cleared). The large nearby hill directly to the west is Jerusalem Mountain, and north of that in the distance is Mt. Greylock, with its long southern ridge and summit crowned with a monument. Possibly visible to the northwest are the mountains of Vermont, including sharp-pointed Haystack and the long ridge of Mt. Snow (its ski trails are visible during ski season).

When you leave the lookout, return to the three-way junction, and turn right. You will now be heading in a southerly direction along the ridge, following both white and blue markers. You will pass a second overlook, not as spectacular as the first, but worth a visit. Continuing on, stay on the main ridge path past the point where the M-M Trail turns off to the right. From here on, the trail is marked with intermittent blue markers. After skirting the edge of a small cliff of overhanging rock topped with dense laurel growth, the trail descends, swings to the right and meets Jerusalem Road again. Turn left here.

Although you may encounter a car along this lane, there is still much solitude here deep in the forest, and you are just as likely to meet some wild turkeys. At a road junction, about 1/4 mile ahead, bear right onto the gated road. From here, walk another 1/4 mile under tall pines overlooking an open, wet area to your left. Soon the road will become paved, bringing you down to Ruggles Pond and the parking area. For those that wish to hike longer, there is a 1.5-mile circular trail around Ruggles Pond. Marked in blue, the trail begins on the pond's east shore, just before reaching the beach.

Vista from the Metacomet-Monadnock Trail

26

Poet's Seat and Sachem Head

Rating: Easy to moderate — a double looped ("figure-8") hike along steep escarpments, through deep woods and on paved roads.
Distance: 4 miles
Hiking Time: 2.5 hours
Lowest Elevation: 250 feet; 76 meters
Highest Elevation: 494 feet; 151 meters
USGS Quad: Greenfield
Other Maps: Greenfield Open Space and Recreation Map, Town Map of Rocky Mountain-Highland Park, NEC Pocumtuck Ridge Trail Map

On the east side of Greenfield there is a narrow basalt ridge called Rocky Mountain, which offers some cliff-top hiking and excellent views. Geologically, it is the same formation as the Pocumtuck and the Holyoke Ranges to the south. Rocky Mountain's northern section is known for its Poet's Seat tower, while the southern section includes Highland Park and Temple Woods. All of this land is protected open space which is managed by the Town of Greenfield. In the Highland Park section, a number of cross-country ski trails have been marked; in the northern section a road leads to the tower, but the rest of the land has been left undeveloped. The hike described below is shaped like a figure-8, and it explores most of these two sections of Rocky Mountain.

The Poet's Seat Tower was named for a favorite spot of the Greenfield poet Frederick Goddard Tuckerman (1821-1873), who was a contemporary of Emerson, Hawthorne, and Dickinson. In the year of Tuckerman's death, a wooden tower was built, which was later replaced by the existing stone structure. From its highest level, there is a near-360° view of the surrounding mountains, including Mt. Toby and Pocumtuck Rock to the south.

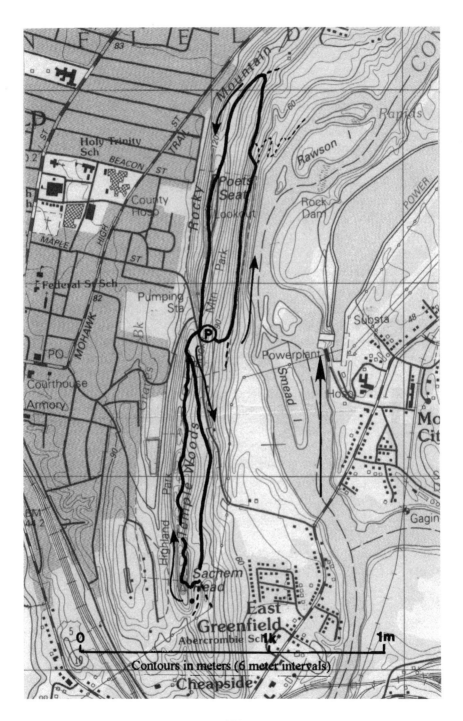

Contours in meters (6 meter intervals)

Trailhead: Approaching Greenfield from the south on Route 5 & 10, cross the bridge over the Deerfield River, and turn immediately right onto Cheapside Street (which turns into Montague City Road), following signs to Turners Falls. After one mile, just before the bridge to Montague City, turn left onto Mountain Road. About 0.9 mile ahead is a turnoff on the right. Park here.

Directions: At the north end of the parking area is a gate and two stone pillars. Just below the pillar on the right (eastern side), there begins a footpath which is marked with red blazes. A wooden sign was recently installed here that reads "Rocky Mountain Loop Trail." Follow the red markers down below the parking area, through bushes and into the woods. At a T-junction with a woods road, turn left and follow the trail through hemlocks and sugar maples along the west side of Rocky Mountain. At a crossing near a power-line structure, the Connecticut River can be seen below.

After another level stretch, the lane narrows to a footpath and then arrives at a junction. One path swings abruptly uphill for a short distance. The other path, the Troop 5 River Trail, continues straight ahead, allowing access to an orange-blazed trail that leads (via switchbacks) down to the Connecticut River. Staying on the red-blazed trail, the steep ascent quickly levels off, and the trail continues heading north, but the walkway here is narrow, more like a deer path. The River Trail bypass rejoins the main trail, which soon widens out to a lane again. After a gradual climb through a hemlock woods, it swings to the left and arrives at a junction with another lane. Bear right, and follow this lane as it swings to the left, arriving at a junction with the blue-blazed Pocumtuck Ridge Trail. Located here is a sign for the red-marked trail that you have been on. Turn left here, now following blue markers, and begin the gradual climb along the summit ridge.

The blue-blazed Pocumtuck Ridge Trail, well-marked and clear, follows the western escarpment of the Rocky Mountain ridge. As you gain in elevation, you pass a few viewpoints of Greenfield near the edge of the cliff. Be careful here, as the drop is considerable. Cedar trees and pitch pines grow in a particularly pleasant stretch of the

The "Bear" on Sachem Head Cliffs

escarpment, where a rock wall crosses the main path. This would be a good choice for a rest stop. Ahead, where the trail swings left as it approaches a bare rock outcrop, leave the trail and climb the rock. Here, just before the tower, are the best views, but the area is also heavily used and sometimes littered.

To leave the tower area, walk south on the paved road. The blue markers will lead off the road and towards a pumping station where markings and trail routes were unclear at the time of this writing. The easiest solution is to turn left here and simply follow the paved road back to the parking area. In about 0.3 mile you will reach Mountain Road, the gate, and (on your left) the parking area nearby. This is the middle of the figure-8. At this point, you can choose to finish your hike or continue onward with the second loop, described below.

Cross the road here, and re-enter the woods on a wide path marked with the blue blazes of the Pocumtuck Ridge Trail. In just a few hundred feet, turn left onto a red trail. A sign here indicates that it leads to Bear's Den Road. After a few ups and downs, the red trail first passes a junction with a white-marked trail and then one marked in yellow. You can take either path. The red markers will lead downhill to the gate for Temple Woods and Bear's Den Road. The yellow trail is a short-cut that joins the road about 0.1 mile ahead. Whichever way you choose, turn right onto Bear's Den Road (an old lane closed to motor vehicles). It is named for a small cave that is located beneath some rock outcrops under Sachem's Head.

Follow Bear's Den Road for about 0.5 mile to where the blue markers of the Pocumtuck Ridge Trail come in from the left. Turn right here, and then climb via footpath to Sachem's Head. If you stay on Bear's Den Road for only a hundred feet past this crossing, you will find the bear's den, an extensive basalt fissure cave, located up and to the right of the road near the end of the ridge. After investigating the cave, return to the junction and turn left, following blue markers as the trail goes steeply uphill.

Sachem Head, the narrow point of a long basalt ridge, offers excellent views in all directions except due north. An old wooden viewing platform is found here, as well as two brass caps which are official U.S. survey markers embedded in the stone. The 100-foot cliffs are spectacular but potentially dangerous. When viewed looking north, they seem to form images of both bear and Indian.

When you leave the platform, head north, following the blue-blazed Pocumtuck Ridge Trail that parallels the edge of the cliff. The trail, which never strays too far from the escarpment, offers many more views out to the west. Eastern views are blocked by a thick hemlock-oak forest. Keep left at all intersections. Eventually, the trail passes the junction with the red trail, and straight ahead is Mountain Road. Your car is just to the right. Use caution in crossing the road.

157

27

High Ledges

Rating: Moderately challenging — a steep descent, a long climb, and some trail intersections that will make you think.
Distance: 4 miles
Hiking Time: 3 hours
Lowest Elevation: 886 feet; 270 meters
Highest Elevation: 1397 feet; 426 meters
USGS Quad: Colrain-Shelburne Falls (old series), Greenfield-Bernardston (new series)
Other Maps: Audubon Society sketch map

High Ledges, a 586-acre wildlife refuge owned by the Massachusetts Audubon Society, is located near the town of Shelburne Falls. Although there are several miles of trail within this refuge, most of the visitors won't be found on them; they head straight for the vista overlooking Shelburne Falls, located at the ledges themselves.

The trail system in the refuge leads to some very interesting places — mountain streams, cascades, rock outcrops, swamps, and areas that contain specific plant species. Because it is a refuge and not a park, the High Ledges attracts naturalists, not recreationists. Dogs are not allowed, and neither is smoking. The trail markings in the refuge are disks nailed to trees, and they are either blue or yellow. Regardless of what trail you are on, if you are heading *away* from the entrance lane and the high ledges area, the disks are blue. If you are heading *back,* they are yellow. If you get lost on this hike (which is possible, as there are a number of trail junctions), simply follow yellow markers, and you will return to the starting point or near it. Sketch maps of the refuge are posted at most intersections, and while the map does not show contours, it does give a rough indication of where things are located relative to each other. The hike described below covers a large portion of the refuge, but by no means all of it. You may wish to explore some of the other trails in the area. (You should take note that the West Brook Trail descends the mountain nearly to a paved road below to reach West Beaver Pond and will require a climb back up on the return.) *Note:* There is a $3 entrance fee for non-members (of the Audubon Society).

Trailhead: There are several ways to reach the trailhead from MA-Route 2 west of Greenfield. One way is to take Little Mohawk Road north from Route 2. This is a right hand turn if you are heading west, and is located 5.4 miles west of the traffic rotary where Route 2 crosses under I-91 (Exit 26). This turnoff, which is just past the Mohawk Trading Post, can also be recognized by a sign for the Davenport Sugar House. Little Mohawk Road swings around past the Shelburne Volunteer Fire Department and then heads north.

Travel 1.4 miles north on Little Mohawk Road and then turn left at a junction onto Patten Road. There may be signs for High Ledges here and also for the Davenport Sugar House. Drive another 0.7 mile in a westerly direction now, passing the turnoff for the sugar house at Reynolds Road. Stay right onto Patten Road. You pass a farm and arrive at the top of the hill with fine vistas to the northeast. To your left on the ridge is the tower overlooking Shelburne Falls. The road becomes gravel, and after another 0.7 mile you will find the entrance to High Ledges on your left. There are some mailboxes here, as the entrance is located between private residences.

Turn onto the entrance road which heads west. There is a parking area located about 0.4 mile in on the left (with room for about 4 or 5 cars).

Directions: Walk in a westerly direction on the road, passing a private drive on the right. After about 0.4 mile, you enter a cleared area. Look for a small footpath on the right. Begin hiking on this footpath which starts near the eastern edge of the cleared area at the gate/directory. You are heading north. At about 150 yards east of the gate near a small apple tree, you find the Waterthrush Trail. It follows the eastern edge of the clearing and enters the woods among white birches and pines. From here on, the yellow markers become obvious (be aware that blue markers are found on the *other* side of the trees).

159

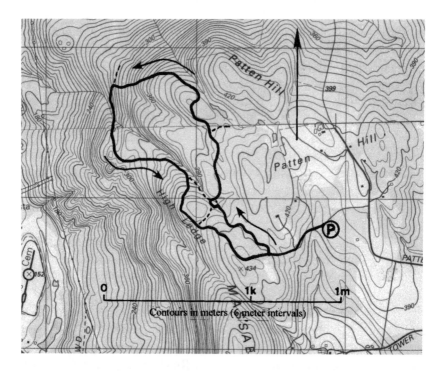

Contours in meters (6 meter intervals)

You pass alongside a wet area loaded with ostrich ferns, then move up to drier area, descend, and eventually meet a brook which the trail crosses twice. If you keep following the markers, you will be led to a trail junction (where a map may be posted) alongside another wet area. From here, you will bear right, now following blue markers, and then after only 100 feet or so, turn right again (small bridge here) near a pump on the Lady-slipper Trail. You are now winding around the wet area and heading back in the direction you came. In another 100 feet, be alert for a sharp left turn where the trail heads north and leaves the wet area. (This description keeps you on the marked trails that circuit the wet area. A short-cut is possible by not making the last brook crossing before entering the wet area, but instead heading straight ahead, then turning sharp right onto the Lady-slipper Trail.)

The Lady-slipper Trail leads up through dense stands of mountain laurel and then down to the Gentian Swamp Trail at a T-junction. Make a right turn here. This trail leads up to a small open area, traversed by a boardwalk. In this area, among the gentians, is a colony of pitcher plants, carnivorous plants that trap and digest insects in their cup-shaped leaves. (You may wish to explore the area ahead which includes a very large wet area off to the left and, much farther down a lane that heads east, an area populated by beaver.) After checking out these plants, turn around and walk back to the edge of the clearing and turn right onto a trail you may not have noticed when you first entered this area. This is the Wolf's Den Spur Trail, and it leads you into a rockier section of the refuge and also to the height of land on this hike. At the top of the rise is an open area with a few rocks to sit on, suitable for a rest or lunch stop. Notice the garnets in the nearby rock.

Continue along the trail, which swings into a northwesterly direction and begins a long descent alongside rock outcrops. The descent steepens and comes to another trail junction at the Wolf's Den area. From here, take the North Trail, which heads west and downhill along a brook, crossing it a few times. Pay careful attention to the trail bed here as well as the markers (still blue on one side, yellow on the other) as it is not a well-used trail. After a long descent through a spooky hemlock forest, you come to a very steep section that ends on an old rock road. Turn left here and begin the long climb back, following North Trail.

The climb continues. You pass alongside a rock wall, crossing to the other side after 150 yards, and continuing the climb in a much drier section of the forest. Here are oaks, ash, maple, and hemlocks. At a junction with the Lady-slipper and Spring Brook Trails, stay to the right (going ahead), and continue climbing in a southerly direction. Openings appear to your right, and you pass another trail junction. Finally, you reach the High Ledges with its great view of the town of Shelburne Falls, a cemetery, a hydro-electric plant, and the Deerfield River Valley.

Located right at the ledges is a private residence, so please respect the owner's rights and privacy. After taking in the vista, walk east past the residence to find the entrance road which will lead you in under 1/4 mile back to the clearing. Continue down the lane to your car.

28

Northfield Mountain

Rating: Moderate — a long climb on a footpath, past cliffs and vistas, to a mountaintop reservoir.
Distance: 5 miles
Hiking Time: 3.5 hours
Lowest Elevation: 343 feet; 90 meters
Highest Elevation: 1,181 feet; 360 meters
USGS Quad: Millers Falls (old series); Orange (new series)
Other Maps: Northfield Mountain Recreation and Environmental Center Trail System map

Northfield Mountain has more uses than any other mountain in the Pioneer Valley. Northeast Utilities, which owns the mountain and some of the surrounding area, uses it as a pump storage electric generation facility. Water is pumped from the Connecticut River to a reservoir on the summit, which is then used as a source of hydro-electric power during peak periods of electric use. Aside from the reservoir, switchyard, and transmission lines, the mountain remains fully wooded, and contains over 25 miles of trails for cross-country skiing, mountain biking, snowshoeing, and hiking. Hunters are also allowed on portions of the mountain. Local schools often bring students here to learn about nature, and orienteering meets are held here regularly. In the fall, cross-country runners from around the state compete here for championships.

There are two types of trails on Northfield Mountain. The network of grassy woods roads are wide enough for two roomy ski lanes and also allow bicyclists enough space to ride aside each other. There are also footpaths which are limited to use by hikers or snowshoers (bikes not allowed), and these are the paths included in the hike described below. At the time of this writing, most of the foot trails were marked with orange tags, but there are also many signs at junctions, most of which are numbered and located on the trail system map. The hike directions may seem complicated (*and they are*), but that is the price to pay for a hiking experience that will be virtually mountain-bike free.

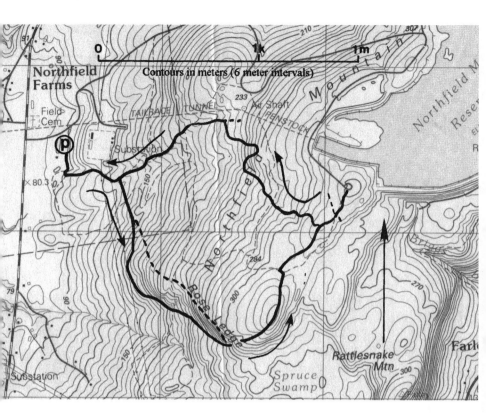

All of the trails on Northfield Mountain are impeccably maintained and a pleasure to hike on. Although there is a charge for skiing here, hikers can use the trails for free. Maps are available at the Visitors Center.

Trailhead: The Northfield Mountain Recreation and Environmental Center is located on the east side of MA-Route 63, about 2.2 miles north of MA-Route 2 near Millers Falls and about 18 miles north of Amherst. From Greenfield, travel about 8 miles east on Route 2, and take Route 63 north for just over 2 miles. Signs will direct you to the Visitors Center, which is on the right side of the road at the base of Northfield Mountain. Park in the parking area adjacent to the Visitor Center. Be sure to visit the Center, which offers tours of the pump storage operation, free maps, and other information about the facility.

Directions: From the parking area, begin your hike by heading in a southerly direction, passing a small pond and the Visitor Center, which will be to your right. You then arrive at an open field. Ahead is a trail sign for the Rose Ledge Foot Trail and the Hidden Quarry Trail which directs you to a footpath. Enter the pine woods here, and begin walking uphill, following blue, diamond-shaped markers. This section of trail is actually part of the Hidden Quarry Trail, used mostly by school groups studying nature, and along the way you'll find a number of informative signs highlighting the natural history of the area. Keep to the left at an unmarked junction, then cross a ski/bike trail and pass under the power-lines. Continue on the footpath, and immediately after a short rise, turn right onto the Rose Ledge Foot Trail, marked with orange, diamond-shaped tags on trees.

Follow the orange markers uphill, and cross first the Hemlock Hill Trail (a ski/bike lane), then a brook with a bridge, and then another ski/bike trail. After a second brook crossing (this one very small and possibly dry), be very alert for an important right turn onto another footpath. Follow this trail, which is the Lower Rose Ledge Foot Trail uphill to an open ledge under power-lines. Here you will find a vista of the surrounding countryside.

Leaving the ledge, the trail passes a rock outcrop on the left and then descends, only to rise again via switchbacks to junction #2 at Yellow Jacket Pass. Cross the ski/bike lane here and continue ahead on the Rose Ledge Foot Trail, where you pass several impressive rock walls which are popular with rock climbers. The trail climbs steadily uphill through this section and then makes a sharp left, just before the last set of cliffs. Using rock steps, the trail swings up and around rock outcrops to arrive at a junction with the Upper Rose Ledge Trail, junction #33.

If you turn left (west) at junction #33 and walk about 100 yards, you will come to several excellent views of distant mountains, including Mt. Greylock. Be careful — these vistas are located along the edge of some very steep ledges. This is also a point where you could shorten your hike. If you wish to turn back now, continue downhill on this Upper Rose Ledge Trail, and it will lead you back to the Quarry Trail and then to the Visitors Center.

Rose Ledges

However, to continue with the complete Northfield Mountain hiking experience, make a right turn at junction #33 and follow the footpath through an oak forest and then out to junction #29. Cross the road here, and continue on the footpath at a more or less constant elevation. Cross another lane and then continue on the footpath, paralleling a ski/bike lane, until you arrive at a paved road. Turn right here and follow signs to a lane that leads down to the Reservoir Viewing Platform. In front of you is the reservoir, full of former Connecticut River water that is ready to be dropped onto turbines when the need for electricity is high. There is also an excellent view from this platform of distant mountains in Vermont, including Stratton and Mt. Snow. When you have seen enough, backtrack to the paved road and to the trail junction. Retrace your steps on the footpath to a crossing of a ski/bike trail. (For a change of pace, from the paved road follow the ski/bike lane called 10th Mountain Trail which parallels the footpath. Make a left at junction #32 and go only 200 feet where you will find your footpath again.)

Continuing to retrace your steps, following the footpath about 200 feet into the woods to the place where another footpath turns right. (You may not have noticed this junction when you passed it heading toward the reservoir). Make a right onto this trail, and begin your descent off the mountain. You will pass a giant solitary hemlock and soon cross another ski/bike lane. Continue downhill to junction #11 and turn right onto the West Slope Trail, another footpath. Follow this beautiful trail as it goes under hemlocks and over and along small brooks. Cross another ski/bike trail, and follow the footpath down and around the back of a small building and several picnic tables. During skiing season, this is the hot chocolate stand. Continue downhill, cross one ski/bike lane and then another at the site of the Hidden Quarry. Cross this lane also and continue downhill, now passing the many descriptive plaques along the Hidden Quarry Trail. Not far ahead you will pass the junction with the Rose Ledge Foot Trail and pass under the power-lines. Take your choice here — the footpath or the wide ski/bike lane. Either one will take you down to where a right turn will lead to the Visitors Center and your car.

29

Mount Tully

Rating: Easy to moderate. The first section involves a steep climb which may not be appreciated by small children or anyone who is out of shape.
Distance: 1.5 miles
Hiking Time: 1 hour
Lowest Elevation: 660 feet
Highest Elevation: 1,123 feet
USGS Quad: Northfield/Winchenden (metric)
Other Maps: Tully Trail Map

Tully Mountain is the focus of the 18-mile Tully Trail which loops through several protected lands in Athol, Orange, and Warwick. The trail passes through the Tully Lake Campground, near to Doane's Falls, over Jacob's Hill, and past Royalston Falls — all of which are managed by The Trustees of Reservations. The northern section of Tully Trail is concurrent with the Metacomet-Monadnock Trail for several miles. It then loops southward through Warwick State Forest and the Tully Mountain Wildlife Management Area, the public land which is utilized in the hike described here. While very serious hikers may be able to hike the entire 18-mile trail in one long day, a more realistic option would be to hike it as a 2-day backpacking trip, using the Tully Lake Campground as one possible spot for camping (make reservations) or a new shelter that is being built on the M-M Trail. The hike described below offers a short introduction to what this region has to offer. The views from the summit are extensive and take in much of the eastern portion of the Tully Trail.

The Tully Trail came about as a result of a coalition of conservation-minded groups that were supported by the National Park Services Rivers and Trails Program. These partners include Massachusetts Wildlife (Department of Fisheries and Wildlife), the New England Forestry Foundation, Harvard Forest, the U.S. Army Corps of

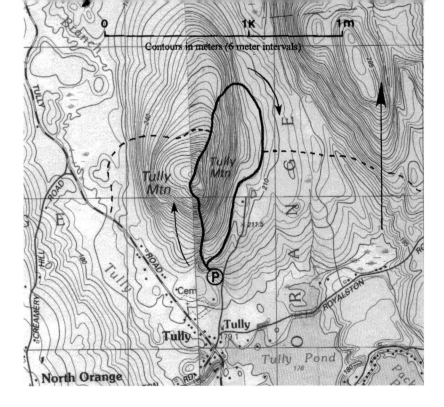

Engineers, Mount Grace Land Conservation Trust, the Massachusetts Department of Environmental Management, and The Trustees of Reservations. The actual trail management and maintenance is handled by The Trustees and many volunteers. An excellent map of the trail is available from The Trustees and may be downloaded from their website *www.thetrustees.org*.

Trailhead: From Route 2A in Athol, turn north onto Route 32, crossing the Millers River and navigating a few turns before leaving town. Following Route 32 north, you can see Tully Mountain and its ledges on the left as you pass by the fields and ventilation pipes of an old landfill. After 2.5 miles of driving, turn left onto Logan and then after only 0.2 mile, keep left onto Freyville. Drive another 0.9 mile and turn right (north). 0.5 mile ahead in a residential area, at a sign for Royalston Road, bear right; then after 0.1 mile, bear left. The mountain is in front of you now. Follow this road, which is a narrow dirt lane, to the Tully Mountain Wildlife Area sign where there is a small parking area (up to 3 cars) on the left.

Directions: At the back of the parking area, find a footpath that leads directly to a trail junction. This is your starting point as well as return point for the loop. Make a left here, following yellow markers and some square metal tags that designate the Tully Trail. Pass through the opening in a rock wall and begin climbing. The route is a steady and steep uphill climb. As you approach the summit, you will begin to notice rock ledges to your right. An unmarked path on right leads to the lowest of the ledges. But keep on climbing to reach the main ledges of Tully Mountain, where large slabs of bare rock offer 180-degree views.

At the summit there are views to east and north. Mount Monadnock in New Hampshire dominates the northern horizon, and to the east is a view of Tully Lake. Unfortunately, the ledges themselves hold a considerable amount of graffiti. After taking in the great views, continue hiking north on the Tully Trail footpath which is located back about 20 meters from the ledges. Just ahead on the path and to the left is the true summit of the mountain, which is completely wooded. Now the trail begins to head down the north side of Mount Tully on a path that varies from a footpath to a woods road. There is an abundance of hemlock growing on this cool, northern part of the mountain. In an area where there are large number of yellow markings, the Tully Trail turns left, leaving the route you are staying on, and heading north on its way to the M-M Trail. Stay on the lane which first levels out a bit, but then descends steeply as it swings slowly around to the east and then southeast.

Be alert for another trail junction; this one is in an area with fewer hemlocks. Here is where the Tully Trail comes in from Tully Lake. Turn right here, now on the Tully Trail again, and follow its markers. This next section of trail, newly cut, is rough; it climbs to a lane that follows a steady contour south all the way back to your starting point. The walking is easy and pleasant all the way. On the right, look for a very large white pine with a stone trapped in its roots; the stone is being slowly lifted as the tree grows. When you arrive at the starting junction, turn left to find your car.

169

View of Mount Monadnock from the ledges of Mt. Tully

30

Mount Grace State Forest

Rating: Moderately difficult. A steady climb of over 1,000 feet to the summit, followed by a return on snowmobile/mountain bike trails.
Distance: 4 miles
Hiking Time: 3 hours
Lowest Elevation: 551 feet; 168 meters
Highest Elevation: 1,617 feet; 493 meters
USGS Quad: Mt. Grace (old series), Northfield
Other Maps: M-M Trail Guide

Mt. Grace is the focus of Mt. Grace State Forest, established in 1920. Close to the New Hampshire border, this state forest lies in the middle of a vast forested area, and the vista from the tower on its summit reveals very little evidence of human habitation. The summit elevation is just below that of Moore's Hill in the D.A.R. State Forest, but the climb to this summit is more demanding. The Metacomet-Monadnock Trail traverses the forest and passes over the summit of Mt. Grace.

Very little of Mt. Grace State Forest is developed. There is a service road to the fire tower on the summit, and there are two parking areas along MA-Route 78. The southern parking area is near a large field, picnic tables, and a shelter. Further north on MA-78 you pass a series of picnic sites containing some old stone fireplaces. Down the road from these more or less abandoned sites is a small parking area for the Metacomet-Monadnock Trail. Trails on the mountain include the "Round the Mountain Trail," which is a snowmobile trail in the process of being adopted for summer use by the New England Mountain Bike Association. Unfortunately, some of the trails in Mount Grace State Forest are being degraded by motorized off-road vehicles (ATVs and dirt bikes), and in some places by sport utility vehicles — in spite of the signs clearly indicating that such uses are prohibited.

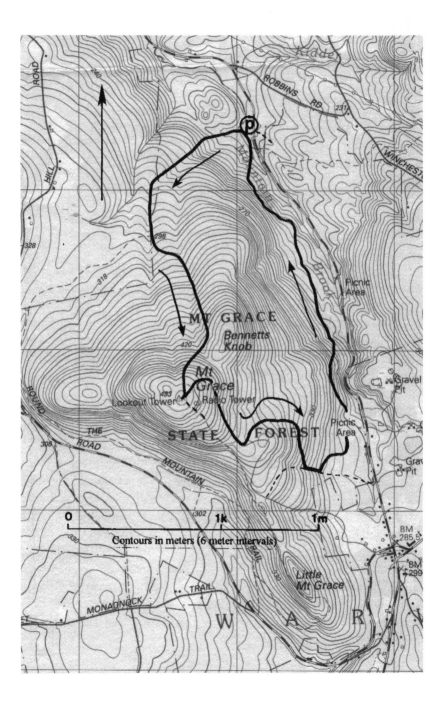

Contours in meters (6 meter intervals)

Trailhead: Mt. Grace State Forest is most easily reached via MA-78 from MA-Route 2A. If you are heading east on Route 2, turn onto 2A at a point about 7 miles east of Miller's Falls and MA-63 (just past the small town of Erving). Follow 2A for about 2 miles to the junction with MA-78. A unique-looking Chinese restaurant is located at this corner, and there is also a state forest sign. Turn north (left) on MA-78 and travel 6 miles to the small town of Warwick. About 1/2 mile beyond the crossroads in this town is Mt. Grace State Forest headquarters and the first parking area. Further north on 78 (now heading downhill), you will pass the brook-side picnic area, and at about 1.3 mile from the forest headquarters, again on the left, the M-M trail crossing. This point is not marked and you may easily miss it. Look for white M-M markers on a utility pole, a speed limit sign, and two small turnoffs on the west (left) side of the road about 150 feet from each other. There is no official parking area here, though there are places for several cars.

Directions: From the trailhead, follow the white markers of the M-M trail, going west into the forest on a rocky road that immediately begins to climb. In less than 1/4 mile you cross over a brook and pass a camping shelter. The trail continues to the left of the shelter, climbing at a steady pace. You pass over two small brooks (not always running) and then, after about 45 minutes of walking, you come to a place where the trail divides. Continue straight ahead on the official route of the M-M Trail. From here, the trail becomes a footpath and the uphill grade steepens. After passing a trail coming in from the left and passing under some dark hemlocks, the flat summit area is reached — a great place for lying around in the sun or under shady white pines and having lunch or a snack. This 1.5-mile climb from the trailhead to the summit should take about an hour, depending on how many times you pause for a rest.

At the summit there is a fire tower that offers extensive views over mostly forested mountains. To the northeast, Mt. Monadnock towers over everything else. Mt. Ascutney is visible to the north, and the Green Mountain range from Killington to Haystack forms a line from the north to the northwest. During ski season, you can see the ski trails on the slopes of Mt. Snow and Haystack. Mt. Greylock and its summit monument are visible to the west. To the southwest you can see Crag and Northfield Mountains and Mt. Toby (just behind this, and against more distant mountains, are the two Sugarloafs). A profile of Mt. Tom is visible, but the top of Mt. Norwottuck is all that can be seen of the Holyoke Range. Due south is a unique view of the Quabbin Reservoir, and to the southeast is Mt. Wachusett. Just below the fire tower is a large boulder that contains a dedication plaque and a USGS survey marker.

After your visit to the summit area, leave the way you came in but prepare for an immediate right turn onto an unmarked service road. Follow this road, ignoring the lane coming in from the right in 100 meters. After about ten minutes walk on this road, you come to a section where the descent flattens out a bit, and you turn left onto a path. (This path starts just before the service road that you are on makes a sharp left and heads more down steeply downhill again. The path you want to take now is indicated by markers on trees, and there may also be a small rock cairn marking this junction.)

Follow this path downhill through a recently cleared forest. It will first head to the northeast and then swing into a more easterly direction. After about 15 minutes of walking, you come to a junction with another woods road, which may be very muddy and eroded from motorized vehicle abuse. However, just before reaching this junction, there is an unmarked (and non-muddy) path that runs parallel to the road. You want to turn left onto this path. Just a short distance ahead, be prepared to turn left again onto the next woods road. This path, which heads north, leads to the open field of the first parking area. Continue walking north along the extreme western edge of the field, and re-enter the forest on a snowmobile/mountain bike trail.

For the next 20-30 minutes, follow this trail, which is mainly downhill (although there are a few short climbs along the way). It parallels MA-78, which you can hear and see at times on your right through the trees. At one point, the trail crosses a small stream on logs. Along the way you will pass several side trails coming in on the left and some structural remains of an abandoned downhill ski area. A little further, the trail meets the M-M Trail; turn right here to find your starting point. Your descent from the summit, a distance of about 2.5 miles, should take about an hour if you make no stops.

Sources for Maps

U.S. Geological Survey Maps (USGS)

The topographical maps used as base maps for the hikes in this book are available from many local booksellers or outfitters for about $6.00 each. Each map covers a specific quadrangle (quad) which is named and shown on a state base map. Beginning in the mid 1980s, a new, updated series of USGS maps has been produced, covering twice the area of the older quadrangles. Currently, these 7.5 x 15 minute quadrangle maps, which show elevations and distances in meters, are available for much of Western Massachusetts. These maps come folded. Maps for the central and southern section of the Pioneer Valley are still available, but only in the older 7.5 x 7.5 minute format, unfolded. You can order these maps from the sources below. Write, call or go online to find out current prices and availability.

www.topozone.com

U.S. Geological Survey
>Box 25286, Denver, CO 80225
>800-ASK-USGS
>*www.usgs.gov/*

Earth Science Information Office
>Blaisdell House, University of Massachusetts
>Amherst, MA 01003
>(413) 545-0359
>*www.umass.edu/+ei/esio*

Casimir Pinigis
>55 Ella Street, Athol, MA 01331
>(978) 249-8486

New England Cartographics
>PO Box 9369, North Amherst, MA 01059
>(413) 549-4124

A.J. Hastings, newsdealers
>45 So. Pleasant St., Amherst MA 01002
>(413) 253-2840

Massachusetts Department of Environmental Management (DEM)

As of 2003, the DEM is still offering free printed maps for most State Forests, Reservations and Parks. These are not very detailed, but they do show hiking trails, and they are free and available at each site. Until recently, you could also send an SASE to the DEM and request that certain maps be mailed to you. However, all of this may have changed by the time you read this. At the time of this writing (2003), the status of these maps was uncertain because the DEM was in the process of restructuring itself into a new Department of Conservation and Recreation (DCR).

According to some sources at DEM, there will be no more printing of maps as it is "more cost-effective" to offer the maps online. You can find these maps at *www.state.ma.us/dem/4parks*. However, you may still be able to find old copies of printed maps at each site, at least until they run out. For information about current organizational changes (DEM, DCR), contact *www.state.ma.us/dem/index.htm*.

New England Cartographics (NEC)

New England Cartographics publishes trail maps for the Quabbin, Mt. Tom, Holyoke Range State Park (east and west), Mt. Toby, and the Sugarloafs. These are excellent quality contour maps designed for hikers. The maps contain plenty of technical information about the various trails as well as historical facts about each area. Each map costs $5.00, postpaid.

New England Cartographics
> PO Box 9369, North Amherst, MA 01059
> (413) 549-4124
> *www.necartographics.com*

Amherst Conservation Commission (ACC)

The Guide to the Robert Frost Trail ($7.95) is available from the Amherst Conservation Commission. The ACC also offers a topographic map which shows the RFT plus all of the Amherst conservation areas ($10.00). Individual maps of 19 different areas are $5.00 each. These can also be purchased at some local bookstores, outfitters, Hastings (see address above), and the Hitchcock Center for the Environment in Amherst.

Amherst Conservation Services, Town Hall, Amherst, MA 01002
> 413-256-4045
> *www.amherstcommon.com/recreation/rftrail.html*

New England Orienteering Club (NEOC)

These are highly detailed topographic maps designed for competitive orienteering. They are available for several areas covered in this guide, including Forest Park, Holyoke Range (East), Mt. Tom, Quabbin Hill, and Northfield Mountain. These colored maps display many features not found on other maps, including large boulders and abandoned trails, and are recommended for very experienced map users. For up-to-date information and prices, contact:

New England Orienteering Club
    48 Holbrook St., Jamaica Plain MA 02130
    781-648-1155
    www.newenglandorienteering.org/

Belchertown Conservation Commission

The topographical Belchertown "Open Space and Recreation" Map is available at the Town Hall for $2.00. A portion of the M-M Trail is shown on this map.

Belchertown Conservation Commission
    Town Hall, Belchertown, MA 01007
    413-323-0405

Other Useful Guidebooks

AMC Massachusetts and Rhode Island Trail Guide. Appalachian Mountain Club. Boston, MA: AMC, 2003.

Metacomet-Monadnock Trail Guide. Original composition by Walter M. Banfield. Amherst, MA: Berkshire Chapter AMC Trails Committee, 2003.

Fifty Hikes in Massachusetts. John Brady and Brian White. Woodstock VT: Backcountry Press, 2003.

Amethyst Brook in winter

Local Nonprofit Conservation and Recreation Organizations

Hiking Clubs and Trail Maintaining Organizations

Appalachian Mountain Club: Berkshire Chapter
    PO Box 9369, North Amherst, MA 01059
    www.amcberkshire.org/

Friends of the Holyoke Range, Inc.
    PO Box 728
    South Hadley, MA 01075
    http://fomhr.tripod.com/

Friends of Quabbin, Inc.
    Quabbin Visitor Center
    PO Box 1001, Belchertown, MA 01007
    413-323-7221
    www.friendsofquabbin.org/

Green Mountain Club
    4711 Waterbury-Stowe Rd.
    Waterbury Center VT 05677
    802-244-7037
    www.greenmountainclud.org

Massachusetts Audubon Society
    208 South Great Road
    Lincoln MA 01773
    781-259-9500
    www.massaudubon.org/

Metacomet-Monadnock Trail Comm.
    PO Box 9369
    North Amherst MA 01059
    http://users.crocker.com/~mmtrail/index.html

Pioneer Valley Hiking Club
    www.geocities.com/pvhcweb/
    c/o Wilderness Experiences Unlimited
    PO Box 265, Southwick MA 01077

Sierra Club, Pioneer Valley Chapter
  100 Boylston St.
  Boston, MA 02116
  617-423-5775

Springfield Explorer's Club
  15 Bruuer Ave.
  Wilbraham, MA 01095

Springfield Naturalist Club
  c/o The Museum of Science
  236 State St., Springfield MA 01103
  http://naturalist-club.org/

Town of Amherst Trails Committee
  c/o Pete Westover
  Conservation Department, Town Hall
  Amherst, MA 01002

Land Trusts

The Kestrel Trust
  PO Box 1016
  Amherst, MA 01004
  413-863-3221

Mt. Grace Land Conservation Trust
  1461 Old Keene Rd.
  Athol MA 01331
  978-248-2043
  www.mountgrace.org/

Nature Conservancy: Mass. Field Office
  205 Portland St., Suite 400
  Boston MA 02114
  617-227-7017

Rattlesnake Gutter Trust
  PO Box 195
  Leverett, MA 01054

Trustees of Reservations
572 Essex Street
Beverly, MA 01915
978-921-1944
www.thetrustees.org

Valley Land Fund, Inc.
PO Box 522
Hadley, MA 01035
413-863-3221
www.valleylandfund.org

AMC Adopt-A-Trail Program

For more information about this volunteer program and how you can become involved, contact the AMC at:
www.outdoors.org/trails/volunteer/adopt/index.shtml

High Ledges (Hike #27)

References

Bain, George W., and Howard A. Meyerhoff. *The Flow of Time in the Connecticut Valley: Geologic Imprints.* Springfield, MA: Connecticut Valley Historical Museum, 1963.

Berkowitz, Steven, ed. *Holyoke Range: History, Resources, Land Use.* Amherst, MA: Hampshire College, 1974.

Conuel, Thomas. *Quabbin: The Accidental Wilderness.* Lincoln, MA: Massachusetts Audubon Society, 1981.

Fuller, Linda K. *Trips and Trivia; A Guide to Western Massachusetts.* Springfield, MA: Springfield Magazine, 1978.

Greene, J.R. *The Creation of the Quabbin Reservoir: The Death of the Swift River Valley.* Athol, MA: The Transcript Press, 1985.

Jorgensen, Neil. *A Guide to New England's Landscape.* Chester, CT: Pequot Press, 1977.

Judd, Sylvester. *History of Hadley.* Springfield, MA: H.R. Hunting. 1905.

Kellogg, Lucy Cutler. *History of Greenfield.* Greenfield, MA: 1931.

Konig, Michael, and Martin Kaufman, editors. *Springfield, 1636-1986.* Springfield Library and Museums Association: 1987. See "Springfield's Indian Neighbors," by Peter A. Thomas.

Little, Richard D. *Dinosaurs, Dunes, and Drifting Continents: The Geohistory of the Connecticut Valley.* 3rd edition. Greenfield, MA: Valley Geology Publications, 2003.

Little, Richard D. *Exploring Franklin County: A Geology Guide.* Greenfield, MA: Valley Geology Publications, 1989.

Northeast Utilities. The Northfield Mountain Interpreter. (written and edited by Claudia F. Sammartino). Berlin, CT: Northeast Utilities, 1981.

O'Connell, James C. *Inside Guide to Springfield and the Pioneer Valley.* Springfield, MA: Western Mass. Publishers, 1986.

Pioneer Valley Group of The Sierra Club. *Symposium on the Mt. Tom Reservation.* Holyoke Community College, November 21, 1985.

NOTES

NOTES

NOTES

NOTES

NOTES

NOTES

If you are enjoying *Hiking the Pioneer Valley*,
you will probably want to hike in nearby southern Vermont.
And here is another great guidebook written by Bruce Scofield ...

Hiking Green Mountain National Forest Southern Section
by Bruce Scofield

New England Cartographics   ISBN 1-889787-06-X   176 pages $14.95

Hiking Green Mountain National Forest: Southern Section is a unique introduction to the natural wonders of Southern Vermont. Informative yet entertaining, this book guides the reader to both the popular sites and the little-known destinations, from the evergreen summits of the mountains to the hidden, wild waterfalls; from huge reservoirs to bogs teeming with wildlife. Hikers, walkers, peak-baggers, and backpackers will all find something of interest and value in this comprehensive guide. Filled with accurate topographic maps, photographs, and trailhead directions, this book also tells the story of Southern Vermont through its fascinating history and unusual geology.

What the reviewers say:

This is the indispensable guide for the pathways to our wild hearts in the wild forests and recovering woodlands of the Southern Green Mountains. This guide covers the terrain with ease, providing one-on-one encounters with the trails and paths, natural history and geologic features, spectacular waterfalls and not-to-be-missed views, wildlife and native plants, as well as essential lore on emboldened blackflies. Whether you're a day-hiker with children, an experienced bushwhacker, or a casual "peakbagger" like myself, you'll be reaching for this guide for the nuts-and-bolts on hiking this area -- and for just plain inspiration to get outside.
> Sue Higby, Deputy Director, Forest Watch
> *www.forestwatch.org*

An engaging mix of fact and philosophy; a history lesson as well as a hiking guide. Author Bruce Scofield is always entertaining and educating in his quirky, detailed style. A recommended hiking guide.
> Paul C. Doyle, Jr.
> Nudas Veritas Publications & Vermont Review

Also Available from
New England Cartographics

Maps

Holyoke Range State Park (Eastern Section)	$3.95
Holyoke Range/Skinner State Park (Western Section)	$3.95
Mt. Greylock Reservation Trail Map	$3.95
Mt. Toby Reservation Trail Map	$3.95
Mt. Tom Reservation Trail Map	$3.95
Mt. Wachusett & Leominster State Forest Trail Map	$3.95
Western Massachusetts Trail Map Pack (all 6 above)	$15.95
Quabbin Reservation Guide	$4.95
Quabbin Reservation Guide (waterproof version)	$5.95
Grand Monadnock Trail Map	$3.95
Wapack Trail Map	$3.95
Connecticut River Recreation Map (in Massachusetts)	$5.95

Books

Guide to the Metacomet-Monadnock Trail	$12.95
Hiking the Pioneer Valley	$14.95
Hiking the Monadnock Region	$10.95
High Peaks of the Northeast	$12.95
Great Rail Trails of New Jersey	$16.95
Skiing the Pioneer Valley	$10.95
Golfing in New England	$16.95
Bicycling the Pioneer Valley	$10.95
Steep Creeks of New England	$14.95
Hiking Green Mountain National Forest (Southern Section)	$14.95
Birding Western Massachusetts	$16.95

Please include postage/handling:

$0.75 for the first map and $0.25 for each additional map;
$1.50 for the Western Mass. Map Pack;
$2.00 for the first book and $1.00 for each additional book.

Postage/Handling _____

Total Enclosed _____

(Order Form is on next page)

* Ask about our GEOLOPES -- stationery and envelopes made out of
recycled USGS topographic maps. Free samples available upon request.

ORDER FORM

To order products, call or write:

New England Cartographics
P.O. Box 9369
North Amherst MA 01059
(413) - 549-4124
FAX orders: (413) - 549-3621
www.necartographics.com

Circle one of the following:

Mastercard   **Visa**   **AMEX**   **Check**   **Money Order**

Card Number _____
Expiration Date _____

Signature _____
Telephone (optional) _____

Please send my order to:

Name _____
Address _____
Town/City _____
State _____ **Zip** _____

Visit our web site
www.necartographics.com